Eyes Of The Jaguar

by

Irene R. Siegel

EPB-AW-101
an
ESCHATON BOOK
from

ESCHATON™

PRODUCTIONS, INC.
60 East Chestnut Street, #236
Chicago, IL 60611

ISBN 1-57353-101-4

"In the past, immortality was maintained by the species, but death came to the individual. As one generation would die, the species would change through the next generation. The sick and weak would die off, and the species was kept strong and pure. The evolutionary process happened naturally, and quickly. But technology has changed all that. Now those that would have died still live... technology has cut our connection with nature. We don't have the time anymore to wait for evolution to make us conscious. It is the individual who must make the leap, not the generation. We, as Shamans, the new caretakers of the Earth, must guide our own species through future sight and not wait for the next generation. We have no time to waste."

EYES OF THE JAGUAR

CHAPTER ONE

We all need reasons to get out of bed in the morning, and I was running out of them. I lay in the wintry, early-morning sunshine, counting the wood panels on the roof, listening to the distant drone of traffic. The world getting ready for another day of rushing here and rushing there so that bank accounts would be higher rather than lower. I was losing my patience with all of that. The wood panels on the ceiling were infinitely more interesting.

I valued these few minutes of solitude and peace, and I was upset with myself whenever I would ruin these precious moments by tailspinning into a funk. None of those cars out there speeding along the Long Island Expressway could have a more frenetic pace than mine. I had recently been hired by a New York state psychiatric hospital to do clinical supervision for thirty-five social workers in mental health clinics throughout Suffolk County. In other words, I had been hired to do the impossible. But the pay was good, the prestige stroked my ego, and I hardly had the energy or time to spend staring at bedroom ceilings, contemplating the emptiness of Life As We Know It.

At last I pulled myself up and went about the business of getting dressed, fixing tea, resisting the temptation to look at the little red light on my telephone answering machine. I wasn't in the mood for early-morning emergencies.

I cradled the cup in my hand and felt the pleasant steam drift into my face. Outside the world was white and cold and getting colder. The weather report on the radio predicted more snow by nightfall. Great.

I downed the rest of my tea, grabbed my coat, and left. I snuck a look at the light as I went out. It was blinking, and I ignored it.

Score one for the modern woman.

Carole and Ellie were patiently waiting for me in the clinic conference room. They were talking in an animated fashion when I finally burst through the door, hair flying and pen uncapped.

"You've made it," Carole said.

I nodded. "Barely."

Carole smiled. She was a soft-spoken woman in her mid-forties, with pixie blonde hair framing a glowing round face. She had an inner youthfulness that was always refreshing after the sea of stressed-out, aging faces I normally came in contact with.

I pulled up a chair and took a deep breath. "So! Where are the others?"

"How many were there supposed to be?" Ellie asked.

"Total of six."

Ellie shrugged her shoulders. She was an olive-skinned, large-boned woman, also in her mid-forties. She had thick dark hair that she was always running her fingers through. She wore large rings and bright red earrings to match her necklace. Ellie was a much more dramatic and intense woman than Carole, and her appearance showed it.

While waiting somewhat awkwardly for the other women to arrive, we fell into the casual kind of talk people do. Ellie and Carole had been talking about holistic health, and how the confines of traditional social work made it difficult to truly explore the nature of illness, psychological dysfunction, and roads to true health. I kept my mouth shut for awhile, letting the two women speak. The fact was, I had always had an interest in psychic phenomena and spiritual healing, but it was an opinion I kept safely tucked away from the rest of my more conservative colleagues.

The conversation went on and we all forgot about the business at hand. We exchanged stories in the usual way about various experiences we'd all had, when suddenly Carole froze, her bright round face a study in alarm. Then she clamped her hands over her ears and shut her eyes very, very tightly, the way children do when they exaggerate sleep.

"What's the matter, Carole?" I said.

"Don't you hear it?"

"Hear what?"

"It!"

Ellie and I looked at each other, then back to Carole. I felt my stomach go a little cold at the sudden turn of events. I leaned close and put my hand on her arm.

"What is it?" I said. "Tell me."

"The whistling."

Again I looked at Ellie, concerned. "What whistling?"

At last Carole took her hands from her ears and looked us straight in the eyes. "Someone in the hall was just whistling. I'm so sensitive to it. It happens all the time now, and it's so hostile. I just cringe with fear. I feel as though I'm suddenly in danger and I want to go out there and tell them to stop."

"Whistling . . ." Ellie said. "Who in your life whistles?"

"Nobody," she said.

In the electric silence an image began to form in my head. The image of a man. I neither stopped it nor encouraged it. I simply let the image form as it wanted to. The man was thin, about five foot ten, and had dark, thinning hair and a moustache.

"Carole," I said hesitantly.

She looked up at me with her large, emerald green eyes. "What?"

"Did anyone in your life look like this?" I went on to describe the image of the man in my head, and as I spoke Ellie's eyes grew wider and wider.

2

"My father! You just described my father!"

I swallowed hard, felt the coldness in the pit of my stomach.

"Can you see him?" Carole went on.

"No. Not really. But I have an image of him in my head."

Carole sat back in her chair, took a deep breath, and kept looking at me with wide eyes. Even Ellie was giving me a curious side-glance. We were co-workers, not fortune-tellers, and this sudden and unexpected drop into the spirit world had made us all a bit uncomfortable. Finally Carole cleared her throat and told us of how her father used to whistle just like that, and that he had died not too long ago. It had never occurred to her to put the two things together, but now that it was out on the table she couldn't believe she had ever overlooked something so obvious.

"Are you a psychic?" Carole asked me, somewhat naively.

"No," I smiled. "At least, I've never thought of myself as a psychic in the sense of crystal balls and palm reading. But I always have had a certain . . . feel for things, you know? I meditate . . ."

My voice trailed off. The two women looked at me with both surprise and relief. I picked up my pen and fiddled with it nervously. Shuffled papers. Avoided their eyes. I felt a strange sense of violating some unspecific professional code by opening up like that in front of a couple of co-workers. By stepping beyond the traditional confines of what social workers talk to each other about behind office doors.

At last I forced a smile and opened my notebook and we got down to the business at hand. Ellie and Carole still gazed at me with confused and interested faces. Perhaps it wasn't by chance that no one else had shown up for the meeting.

That night I sat alone in my apartment and listened to the rain and thought about what had happened in the conference room. I thought of Carole's stunned face when I mentioned her father, and how Ellie had given me that sideways glance.

Now -- in the silence and safety of home -- I was able to let myself feel how extraordinary the incident was. Perhaps I was a little blase because my whole life I had been somewhat psychic, and the experiences didn't shock me anymore. But it had been awhile. The delicate antenna that make such experience possible had been dulled by the repetition and common concerns of our day-to-day, anxiety-ridden existences. Our lives get so cluttered we stop paying attention to all that is not "practical," all that won't help towards paying the rent.

I put down my glass of wine and went to the desk in the living-room. Sitting in the same spot where they'd been left months ago were the brochures. The brightly-colored folders of Peruvian mountains and Amazonian jungles, of

Shamans and craftsmen and mysterious lines, ten feet wide, carved into mountainsides.

They were in the drawer for a reason. Handy, but out of sight. It was a temptation I had been avoiding. An inclination I refrained from following. The mature, workaday woman in me protested that one must grind away, even if you start to find yourself staring at the ceiling at night. But now the brochures that lay spread before me were more than just images of a possible future. They called to me. Spoke to me. Breathed into the room a challenge and a promise.

I took a deep breath, gathered them up, and put them back in the drawer.

Monday morning I was sitting in my office when the door burst open and Carole came bouncing in.

"Do you have a minute?" she asked.

"Sure."

Carole closed the door behind her, sat in the chair, and smoothed imaginary wrinkles out of her skirt. "I spent all weekend thinking about how you picked up on my father the way you did. I . . . have you always been able to do this?"

"Yes," I said. "But I'm pretty careful about where and how I use it."

Carole nodded, let her eyes drop to the floor. She was wanting to get to something, but was having trouble. Finally she said, "Do you think it's some sort of psychic message?"

I shook my head. "I have no idea what it was. It came to me, and that was as far as I analyzed it."

Carole nodded some more, obviously not satisfied with my answer. Her eyes scanned my desk, and I saw them stop on a dime.

"What's that?"

She pointed at the brochures of Peru and Brazil I had brought along to the office. I bit my lower lip. Oh, well. Too late to cover them up now.

"It's a long story," I said.

Carole shrugged. "I have all the time in the world."

"Okay." I leaned back in my chair and told Carole the whole chain of events that brought the brochures to my desk in Long Island. "For quite a few years now I've been interested in psychic ability, healing, and exploration. I took a course in psychic development, then enrolled in a week-long workshop in upstate New York that was taught by Dr. Alberto Villoldo. He's a psychologist with a research background, based in California, who has studied Shamanism for over fifteen years in Peru." Carole looked confused, as if I was speaking an unfamiliar language, "Shamanism? what's that?" I tried to maintain my professional stance. "A Shaman is a medicine man or woman, a healer who works with spirit and mediates between spirit and our ordinary world."

"The workshop sounds interesting," Carole said, her eyes brightening.

"It was incredible."

"What made it so incredible?"

"Well . . ." I smiled and looked at the far wall. "Alberto is tall, dark, handsome, young . . ."

Machu Picchu

"That's it," Carole said, laughing. "You don't have to explain anymore. He just met all my requirements for a week-long workshop."

I laughed along and sat up straight, gathering the brochures in my hand. "But seriously, there was much, much more. He took us into the non-ordinary reality of the Shaman through meditation. We learned to connect to our own power source and with our own power animals."

Carole looked at me blankly. "Power animals?"

"Yes." I felt myself fumbling along. I wasn't used to talking about these things. They were special concerns of mine, concerns that I had kept private and close to the vest for a number of reasons, both personal and professional. Also, I felt in my heart that I didn't entirely understand the whole mystical and terribly mysterious world of the Shaman and power animals either, and that my attempts to explain what I felt would inevitably fall short. I fumbled on. "It's difficult to understand, but there is a way to connect with these power sources and use them for healing. For obtaining knowledge."

Carole hadn't taken her eyes off me. They held a stare -- complete, absolute, unwavering. "Can you do this?" she said. "Can you connect with your power animals?"

I stood and walked to the window. "I don't know. I think I have, but it is still very murky . . . I'm not as disciplined or as clear about it as I should be . . . as I want to be. It's like you talk about love, and somebody asks you if you have ever loved like that. You might say yes, but then the future proves you wrong."

I turned from the window and met Carole's relentless and fascinated gaze. "That is why I have those brochures on my desk," I said, gesturing towards the pamphlets. "Every year Alberto takes a small group to Peru, deep into the jungles and high atop the mountains, to study with a very famous Peruvian Shaman. I would love to go some day. There are times when it is all I think about."

Carole stood and continued to slap the wrinkles from her unwrinkled skirt. I suddenly felt foolish and a little afraid. It was not like me to go on about this subject with co-workers.

She walked to the door and didn't say a word, opening it and standing for a moment in the open threshold. Then she turned to face me and her eyes were as serious as any eyes I had ever seen before.

"Go to Peru," she said. "Go."

I cleared my throat. "You think I should?"

The traces of a smile drifted across Carole's face. "Maybe the whistle had more than one purpose." And she turned and left me in the office alone.

CHAPTER TWO

A year passed. I resisted the temptation to plunge headlong into the South American Andes and instead spent the twelve months preparing for my journey. I paid closer attention to those aspects of me that had always seemed incidental in the past.

Even as a child, I had felt my strong spirituality. It did not blend with my family background; New York, conservative, Jewish. Now and then I would talk about my beliefs involving the spirit realm, past lives, and psychic phenomena, and my parents would simply stare at me and say, "Where did you come from?"

Nevertheless, I continued on a relatively traditional path into adulthood. I was a good student, a Girl Scout, a camper, and had plenty of friends. My career choice and my academic accomplishments fit in very well with the goals and expectations of a traditional Jewish family.

So in the year that passed between my visit with Carole in my office and the trip to Peru, I went back to those roots, those early impulses, and gave them the nurturing and attention they had always deserved. I knew that this trip to Peru was not going to be a two-week thing, like a vacation to Hawaii. What would happen to me there would stay with me for the rest of my life. I was not going to take off unprepared.

My preparation meant an immersion in things spiritual. I spoke to various professionals in the field, read voraciously, meditated and tried to keep myself insulated from the million tiny distractions of everyday life.

Finally, one hot and humid morning in mid-August, I walked into Carole's office and announced that I was ready to go.

"To go where?" Carole said.

"Peru."

Silence. Carole put down the file she was editing and stared up at me. "You mean that thing we talked about last year in your office?"

"That's right."

"I thought you'd forgotten about it," Carole said. "That's why I hadn't mentioned it again."

"The time wasn't right then. It is now."

Carole pushed her file aside and rose from her desk. She was still trying to straighten wrinkles from her skirt. Some habits die very hard. "When does it happen?"

"I'm not sure. I'm going to call Alberto in California tonight."

Carole nodded while I spoke. Then she took a deep breath, averted her eyes, and clamped her hands together. "I was wondering," she said. "I was wondering if maybe, you know, I could go with you."

"To Peru?"

She nodded. "I've been thinking about it ever since our talk last year. My problem with the whistling . . ." She trailed off and smiled up at me sheepishly. "I haven't told anybody, but I've gone to a couple of Shamanic workshops, psychic healers . . . you know. I need to work it out. If you were going to Peru I think I would have the strength to make the trip too."

I smiled, reached across the desk and gave Carole a squeeze on the arm. "It would be wonderful to have you come along."

Alberto Villoldo

I found myself oddly nervous while dialing Alberto's number. It had been nearly four years since I had last seen him at the workshop in upstate New York. The adrenaline was pumping. What if he wasn't there anymore? What if his trips to Peru had been discontinued? I suddenly cursed myself for not making sure of these things earlier. My trust was so great that it had to happen that I had neglected to tend to certain basic details. My fears were alleviated when Alberto himself answered the phone. We had a good talk. Yes, the trips were still happening, and yes, he would be happy to have me join him on his next journey to Peru, scheduled for the end of September. I told him about Carole, and her eagerness to come too, and Alberto said it would be fine.

"If you think she is ready for this journey," he said. "Then I will trust your judgement."

I hung up with both excitement and apprehension. The trip was going to happen! And then I thought of Carole the way she was in that conference room a year ago, hands clamped desperately over her ears, trying to keep the whistling out. This journey with Alberto was going to take us to places so strange, to arenas of such untapped power, that I wondered how well Carole would hold up. She was coming because Alberto trusted my judgement. I hung up the phone with my excitement tempered by a deep, unspecified unease. I was not sure of my judgement at all in this case.

The next day at work I went into Carole's office and gave her the good news. She was ecstatic, and some of my apprehensions of the night before were put to rest. There was something solid and dependable about Carole that would see her through whatever we encountered. And it would be nice to share this experience with a friendly and familiar face. In the past year we had become good friends. Carole's bright, perky, creative, and has a wonderful sense of humor. Her humor, I thought, would probably be indispensable to where we were going.

"I'm really going!" she said. "Peru!"

I laughed and sat on the edge of her desk. "Start brushing up on your Spanish."

"A real Shaman . . ." Carole said, thinking about don Riccardo, the Peruvian Shaman Alberto works with. "I wonder how powerful he is."

"We'll soon find out, won't we?"

Carole turned around and swept a hand across her short, slightly overweight body. "Do you think he could do something about this?"

"Your body?" I said. Carole nodded. I shrugged. "What did you have in mind?"

Carole put her finger to her chin and gazed up at the ceiling. "Oh, you know. Tall and thin. Kind of a cross between Sophia Loren and Bridget Bardot."

I climbed off her desk and headed out of the office. "You'd better go easy," I said, smiling. "You're liable to use up all don Riccardo's powers on the first day and leave none for the rest of us."

That night I called Ellie to tell her what Carole and I were up to. There was a pause, and then, to my astonishment, Ellie blurted out her own desire to go on this trip, and did I think Alberto would mind. I told her to call him herself and hung up, a little numb. She called right back and said that she'd spoken to Alberto and it was all set up. The three musketeers! Then she hung up herself and went scurrying to take care of all the last-minute details.

I almost had to laugh. This was sort of like <u>The Wizard of Oz</u>, where Dorothy keeps running into people along the yellow brick road who want to go see the Wizard too.

I went to bed and lay there in the dark, staring at the ceiling. <u>The Wizard of Oz</u> analogy was locked in my head, and the songs played past me, one by one. Everybody wanted something from the Wizard . . . a heart, a brain, courage, to go back home. And I remembered how shocked I had been as a little girl to discover that the Wizard was just a hoax, a little man working knobs on a great machine to give the impression of power and mysticism. I turned in bed, looked away from the ceiling. But they got what they wanted, didn't they? Yes, they did. Of course, they had some luck with the witches along the way. Would I have the same luck with the witches that awaited me? Friends had warned me of Peru, of the political unrest, the militaristic presence. There were many demons to deal with, both tangible and psychic.

I fell asleep and dreamt of munchkins, mean ladies on bicycles, soldiers in helmets, and houses whirling through improbable tornadoes. Then I saw myself wandering through the mountains in a land far, far away. I was frightened, but I kept walking. Just kept walking, right past the danger and things that go bump in the night.

Lions. And tigers. And bears. Oh my.

The time flew by quickly and my excitement rose rapidly. Then, only a few weeks before departure, I got a call from Alberto's office. The trip was postponed by one day, from September 27th to September 28th. I felt tremendously annoyed. I didn't want to wait even one extra day to begin the journey. But I took it in stride and changed the flight reservations. Carole, Ellie, and I were due to fly down to Miami on the 28th and meet the rest of the group. From there we would all fly together to Peru.

Ironically, on September 27th the New York area was hit by hurricane Gloria which immobilized Long Island for the entire day. Fallen trees blocked the streets and power lines were down. There was no electricity and I had difficulty getting a telephone line. I resisted the temptation to attribute Alberto's inexplicable postponement to the anticipation of hurricane Gloria.

The next day, as we drove through the battered streets, avoiding fallen trees and scattered garbage cans, the environment itself seemed to be making an effort to hold us back. The common landscape of Long Island was disheveled, but the one day delay allowed us to slip through and leave the familiar behind. We were journeying to the unknown.

CHAPTER THREE

It was late at night by the time we arrived at the Miami International Airport. Our marathon flight to Peru was not due to depart until after midnight. We found the rest of our group in front of the Faucett Airline Terminal. From a distance, I could see Alberto. He was hard not to see. Tall, thin, with a head full of bushy dark hair, he was easy to pick out of the crowd. He was as handsome and charming as I'd remembered him. I ran over to him, and he gave me a big hug.

"How are you?" he said.

"I'm good. Well . . . mostly good." We both laughed. I turned towards my companions. "Alberto, I want you to meet Ellie and Carole." Ellie and Carole both nodded slightly, smiling nervous, tentative smiles. "The three of us worked very hard preparing for this journey," I went on. "We're all excited, but . . . a little nervous."

Alberto nodded understandingly. "If you weren't a little nervous, you wouldn't be fully prepared for this trip," he said. He started to elaborate on the statement when he was pulled away by other members of the group who had one crisis or another going on. He gave us a what-can-you-do look and went off.

We dragged our heavy luggage over to a waiting area and I spent a moment watching Alberto deal with the other group members. I found myself oddly frustrated, like a little girl who wants everything all for herself. A part of my brain said that this was too important a journey to have to share Alberto with anyone who happened to have confusion over a transfer ticket. I wanted to crawl into his head and learn what he had come to learn through fifteen hard years of studying Shamanism and traveling to the mystical places of the earth. I tapped my fingernails on the wooden chair and kept my frustrations to myself.

But the feelings didn't go away. Then I remembered that when I first met Alberto, he had told the group that we all have our own power. We should not look to him as a guru, but find the guru, or Shaman, within ourselves. Yet I couldn't help but link my spiritual growth to him. The sense of power emanating from him was enormous, and I couldn't resist the temptation to get close, to siphon off some of his power and use it for myself. I was doing with Alberto what I had done with so many men in my life. I wanted to give my power away to him.

Throughout my life I have looked towards men to be protectors and teachers. It was natural. Or so I was taught. My father was a very bright and successful attorney. He supported the family while my mother stayed home to take care of me and my younger sister. The breadwinner and the child-rearer. And my mother played along perfectly into the scenario. She taught my sister and I that men were smarter and wiser and had power and that women were needy and dependent and inadequate. We would do well to follow her example.

And now here I was, starting to do the same thing with Alberto, the one man I knew of on the planet who could help me realize my own power. I smiled to myself and quit tapping the wooden chair. I was learning already. The plane didn't have to touch down in Peru for the journey of awakening to begin.

The flight to Peru was long, but painless. It gave me a chance to size up the other members of the party. There were twenty-two of us in all, and I recognized several from the workshop I had taken with Alberto a few years earlier. There was Sadie -- a bundle of frenetic energy, exuding enthusiasm to all of us on the plane. She'd brought along her own pot so she could do her personal microbiotic cooking. There was Lynn, a fair-skinned, youthful grandmother with tons of luggage and a different earring in each ear. Then there was Vicki, Alberto's young assistant. She, too, wore a big smile and unsuppressed enthusiasm. I felt good. This was going to be a good trip.

Somewhere over the dark continent the woman sitting next to me leaned over and spoke. Her name was Madison, a well-known psychic healer in the United States. A beautiful woman in her sixties, Madison had high cheek-bones, delicate features, and a mound of golden brown hair piled upon her head.

"I have a very good friend who works for the State Department," she said.

"Oh?"

"He told me something before I left."

I leaned closer. "What was that?"

"He said that more Americans disappear from Peru that from any other country in the world."

I just looked at her. For a moment I couldn't decide what Madison meant. Was she speaking in the here-and-now, referring to the volatile political climate of Peru, or was she saying something else? More Americans disappear from Peru than from any other country in the world. Was it a warning . . . or a veiled promise of good news to come?

I leaned my head back on the airline seat and shut my eyes. Time would soon tell. This particular American was ready to "disappear."

I don't know what I was expecting, but it wasn't what I found in Lima.

We landed at seven o'clock in the morning and fought our way through hordes of Peruvians who swarmed at us, begging for money or attempting to sell cigarettes. Alberto had planned ahead, however, and a bus was right there to whisk us out of the chaos.

12

As we rode I stared out the yellowed window and shook my head. This was not how the brochure looked. This was not how I had imagined the launch pad for the soon-to-be spiritual ascent. The city of Lima looked brown. There was very little grass and all the buildings looked dirty and run-down. We passed small stucco homes crammed together, naked children out in the front, metallic-looking water dripping from community faucets. Graffiti was everywhere. Gray, leaden clouds hung low. I clenched my hands and wondered what I had gotten myself into.

Lima: Hotel Bolivar

Alberto must have anticipated the general shock that his various groups went under at the first sight of Lima, so it was with great relief that the bus turned a corner and a fairy-tale castle lay before us. Well, it wasn't exactly a castle, but it certainly looked that way at the time. It was the Grand Hotel Bolivar, which Alberto announced was the most beautiful hotel in all of South America. I walked up the marble steps into the lobby. A huge crystal chandelier hung high above the clusters of leather love seats and marble tables. I took a deep breath and let it go. You can take the girl out of the city, but you can't take the city out of the girl. I was ready for a tea and pastry. Indulge myself. For the journey was going to grow very strange from here.

I spent my free time in Lima perusing the city, particularly the Golden Museum. It was a beautiful museum with many Peruvian artifacts from ancient civilizations. Carole, Ellie, Ralph, Diego, and Bruce came with me to the museum.

Bit by bit I was coming to meet and learn about my companions on this trip. Ralph was the improbable owner of a construction business who, at the age of thirty-nine, decided there must be a better path. This was his attempt to discover it. He was a gentle man -- witty and loving and kind, and I found myself hoping that he stumbled across the path he sought.

Diego -- though a native Peruvian -- looked very Nordic. At twenty-two years of age he was the youngest in the group. He had come all the way from his adopted country of Switzerland for this trip. He was a student in Europe but was here in his original country in search of something. He wasn't sure what it was. A hunch.

Bruce was a psychologist from California, and embodied everything I had always associated with West Coasters. He was blonde, tan, hip, and inclined towards instantaneous friendship.

Towards the end of our visit to the museum Bruce suddenly called to us.

"Hey," he said. "Come over here and take a look at this."

We wandered over. Bruce was standing in front of a ceramic mask hanging on the wall.

"What's so exciting?" I said.

"The $64,000 question," Bruce said. "Who does this face remind you of?"

Our smirks fell away. Each of us gasped in astonishment. Ralph and Diego wandered over to investigate the excitement.

"What's happening?" Ralph said.

"Look at this mask!" Ellie cried out. "It's your face, Ralph! It's you!"

The mask was hundreds of years old, but the model for it could have been standing right next to us. Even Ralph's face went slack with amazement.

"I have to get a shot of this," Ellie said excitedly, unstrapping her camera. "Get under it, Ralph. Let me get a side by side photo."

Ralph willingly accommodated her, and we all laughed nervously at the eerie set of circumstances. The camera flashed, we applauded self-consciously, and Ralph moved away from the mask with a sheepish smile on his face.

We spent another fifteen minutes in the museum, and as we were leaving I noticed Ralph hanging back. He had gone back to the mask, alone, and was standing before it in a strange kind of communion. I took a deep breath, left it as it was, and turned to go back to the hotel and whatever came after.

That evening we gathered as a group for our first meeting with Alberto and don Riccardo Caldez in a small meeting room adjacent to the hotel lobby. I was very anxious to finally meet Alberto's illustrious Shaman friend. As I took my seat in the circle of chairs I curiously looked over at don Riccardo. He was sitting quietly next to Alberto with his arms folded and resting on his large, protruding belly. This was a Shaman who liked to eat. His jet black hair was pulled back and pinned into a knot, and a thick black mustache extended down the side of his dark, round face. He wore blue jeans and a T-shirt. He did not fit my image of such a master. But then, this trip was meant to discard my preconceived "images" of people and things.

Don Riccardo did not speak much English, so Alberto did the translating. Alberto had studied with don Riccardo for fifteen years, and though he was never called "The Master," in an outright fashion, it was always implied. The words did not have to be spoken.

When don Riccardo began to speak his imposing image dissolved. He exuded warmth and compassion and down-to-earthness. His dark brown eyes twinkled and his laughing smile reached from ear to ear. Alberto translated as don Riccardo spoke.

"We're beginning the first phase of the journey," he said. "We will be taking the same steps as the original Shamans took on their journey of initiation."

As he spoke I felt the excitement build within. I glanced at Carole and Ellie and they returned my look. We were a long way from that board room in New York.

"We will use the Medicine Wheel as a learning tool," don Riccardo went on. "Just as the Shamans have done for ages. We are going to be calling on the spirits of the Four Winds to guide us through our journey. We will travel to each direction of the Medicine Wheel and call upon the spirit of that direction. In the South, the Serpent. In the West, the Jaguar. The Eagle, in the East. And to the North, the Horse.

Again, I let my eyes scan the room. Everyone was fixated on don Riccardo as he gracefully illustrated his words with his hands. He spoke so eloquently he all but summoned up the spirits in to the lobby of the Grand Hotel Bolivar. The pitch of his voice was the music to the dance he was creating.

"These are the archetypes of the nature world," he went on. "The original energy forms from which all else in nature has been modeled. Calling upon these spirits allows us to tap into an ancient historical image of very wise energy forms. It's very important to bring the archetype into the moment and connect with it deeply. And the way to do this is by giving it form."

Alberto could sense the slight confusion in the room as we struggled to grasp the concepts of don Riccardo's speech. "It is a cleansing process in the beginning," Alberto said. "We will travel to the south of Peru and go through the rituals that will help to cleanse us. We will call upon the Serpent to help disconnect us from our past life karma and to set us free on our path. One cannot build without sweeping away the clutter of what existed before." Alberto paused, smiled a comforting smile. "Are you following me?" Nervous laughter drifted through the room. We did, and we didn't.

Alberto went on. "Then we will travel to the West and call upon the Jaguar to help us die. We will go through a spiritual death and a spiritual rebirth. The Rainbow Jaguar has its hind legs in the physical and his forelegs in the spiritual realm. We will go through the rituals which will help us prepare to die. Just outside of Cuzco there is a sacred initiation site where we will go to ask to die and to again be reborn as a Shaman, an Inca, a child of the Sun."

"Then we will travel to the East and we will call upon the Eagle to help us create a vision for ourselves. We will look ahead to the future and create our destiny for ourselves and for our planet."

"And, finally, we will travel to the North, and call upon the Horse to take us to the Crystal Cave where the Masters sit and we will sit among them and ask them to teach us of the higher knowledge."

"We will take this journey together. We will all follow the path that Shaman have followed for centuries in the initiation process. But we may not all get initiated. Don Riccardo will initiate only those who he feels are fully prepared to accept the responsibilities that go with becoming a Shaman, a caretaker of the Earth."

I felt my heart pounding as I considered the seriousness of the initiation process. This was not like America, where you pay your money and the goods are handed over. Nothing was promised here. Nothing guaranteed. This would require a commitment as I had committed to nothing in the past.

Carole was sitting next to me and began tugging on my arm.

"What?" I whispered.

"Do you think this will cure my 'empty nest' syndrome?"

I smiled and put my hand on her arm. "Be quiet!"

"The Shaman," Alberto explained. "Has in many ways been a tribal leader in the past. A Shaman will heal on many levels; the mind, the body, and the spirit. Unlike Western doctors, who identify a problem and treat a symptom, the Shaman works with the whole person on many levels at once, integrating the mind, body, and spirit in the healing process. The act of diagnosis and healing are one and the same for the Shaman. The Shaman believes that we in the West live in a cultural trance. If we are symptom-free we think that everything is well and fine, but in truth we are really stagnating. It order to change and grow, we must experience dis-ease. So what we label as illness and view in negative terms, the Shaman views as an opportunity for growth. We try not to rock the boat. The Shaman wants to rock it. We must break through our own cultural trance."

"See, Carole," I whispered to her. "It was your whistling problem that led you on your spiritual path. If it wasn't for the problem, you wouldn't be here. Look at what your 'problem' made possible!"

"You're right," she said, contemplating the chain of events for the first time. "But there's a larger question here."

"What's that?"

"If I become a Shaman, can I make myself tall and thin?"

Alberto continued to talk, giving us an overview of the Shaman and what we could expect in the coming days. A Shaman, he explained, doesn't just deal with physical ailments, but extends his powers and influence to include problems in the community and dysfunction in emotional and interpersonal relationships. And as Alberto spoke, I thought how closely the role of the Shaman in his tribe correlated to the position of a Social Worker in modern society. In school, I was taught that social work deals with every system that effects the client in an effort to facilitate growth and improve the quality of life. This includes the intrapsychic and interpersonal, as well as taking into account the community, family and both physical and emotional system of the individual. So why not the spiritual? It seemed a natural progression of my social work training. To explore the roots of Social Work, it may mean exploring the role of the original Shaman. I was amused by the irony. My professional training, so rigorously opposed to this realm of healing, was the very thing that led me to the marble walls of the Grand Hotel Bolivar.

"The earth is dying," Alberto said in summation. "We have little time to waste. A few years ago don Riccardo had a vision that the new Shamans, the new caretakers of the earth, would come from the West. Our waters are polluted, our jungles are virtually destroyed, and species are becoming extinct. We must take a quantum leap in consciousness in order to heal the earth. In the past, a generation had to die in order for a more advanced form of the species to develop. We don't have that kind of time anymore. With science advancing as quickly as it has been, each generation is living longer. Now a new species of man must develop within a generation. Within our lifetime."

There was a real sense of urgency in Alberto's voice. An urgency I hadn't heard before. I was ready. Ready to learn, ready to take that quantum leap. As far as I was concerned, I couldn't learn fast enough.

CHAPTER FOUR

Our journey to the South began early the next morning. Carole, Ellie, and I had decided overnight to be roommates for the duration of the trip. I was used to living alone, and I went into this arrangement with some trepidation. But I sensed that it would be important to have someone to share the coming experiences with. Someone who would be there in the middle of the night.

The bus ride to Paracas was brutal. Five bumpy hours along dusty dirt roads. Even when the terrain changed from flatland to mountain, the color stayed the same. Brown. Always brown. I felt my spirits sag and wondered how the people of Peru could survive off this land.

In the midst of my gloomy meanderings, Sadie -- the forty-ish woman who had packed her own rice pot -- came and sat down beside me. We chatted for a few minutes about this and that, and then I asked her why she had come all the way to Peru for this bizarre and unknown journey.

Sadie smiled, "What else? A man."

"Only that?" Sadie shook her head. "Well . . . no. Not entirely anyway. I've been in a relationship for over three years now with a man who seems utterly incapable of making a commitment."

"Three years isn't too bad," I said, trying to make her feel better. She was smiling, but there was a sadness in the smile.

"Oh, he's logged the time, but it hasn't been a good three years, if you know what I mean. It's been three years out on the periphery. We can't get close." Sadie stopped, took a deep breath, exhaled. "So that's my sad story. He's planning to move out and leave the country for awhile. Probably packing up his things as we speak." Sadie smiled a bitter smile. "I'm not expecting him to come back and I'm not going to sit crouched in front of the door wagging my tail in anticipation. But it hurts. It hurts a lot. I made him too important in my life, and now I feel as though part of me is lost and dying."

"Is that why you're here?" I asked.

Sadie nodded. "Mostly, I guess. I want to find that part of me again."

"I know what you're going through," I said. "I know how it feels to make a man so important in your life, and then to be disappointed." I smiled, shook my head, and leaned close to Sadie. "To tell you the truth, I think I'm doing it right now, all over again."

"You're kidding!"

"I'm not. I've been thinking about how much power I'm giving to Alberto on this trip. From the moment I first set eyes on him at the airport in Miami."

Sadie nodded understandingly. "He's an easy person to give your power to."

"Exactly. My spiritual growth has become so important to me, and Alberto seems to have so many answers . . . I'm impatient, and I'm approaching him with such awe that I can barely speak. It's silly!"

We both laughed and looked around to see if anybody else was listening in to our conversation.

"Listen," I said, putting a hand on Sadie's arm. "If at the end of this trip I can relate to Alberto as just one of the gang, I will have really accomplished a lot."

Coastal Desert

The ride went on, and the bus was filled with music and chatter. I got to know many of my fellow travelers. There was Al and his wife, Annette. They were so much in love it almost overwhelmed me. I felt wonderful to be surrounded by the flow of their energy. He was a gentle man, and he spoke of the clinic he ran back in Colorado.

At some point Bruce broke out the ten pound sack of raisin and nut mix and began sharing it with the group. The food got us going. Bruce stood up suddenly and began dancing in the aisle of the bus. We all laughed, and one by one others followed.

I resisted, as my natural shyness always makes me resist, then suddenly I was unable to contain myself. I jumped up into the aisle and began to dance. Before long, the entire group was forming a conga line in the aisle of the bus. Alberto stayed in his seat at the front, laughing and cheering us on.

We were united. We were beginning to come in touch with that strong sense of being a tribe.

All dirt roads eventually end. At least, that's what I learned long ago in geography. But this one threatened not to. So it was with enormous relief that we rounded a bend and the tires hit concrete and the Hotel Paracas lay shimmering before us like the Emerald City.

Paracas is a beautiful resort area, right on the edge of a gorgeous bay, surrounded by palm trees. Alberto told us as we disembarked that there would not be a lot of leisure time on the trip, so we should really take advantage of the free time we had that afternoon.

I, of course, was having none of it. If I wanted to sit around a pool, I would have gone the Bahamas. Shamanism was the one and only thing in my mind, and restlessness at postponing the business at hand grated at me. Alberto smiled at my impatience.

"The Shaman can't always be serious," he told me, putting a hand on my shoulder. "You have to be able to take yourself lightly, which means to keep your sense of humor and have some fun."

They eat dinner very late in Peru, and before the ten o'clock meal we all gathered in the bar of the Hotel Paracas and had Pisco Sours. It was a tangy, powerful drink. I stood somewhat apart and watched, wondering why I had been asked to prepare for this trip by restricting my diet and abstaining from alcohol. I'd been a good girl, purifying myself, and now here I was, sitting in a bar watching the booze flow like water. I remembered a Zen proverb. Before Zen, a mountain is a mountain. During Zen, it's all mixed up. After Zen, a mountain is a mountain. I was in stage two, and the concept of paradox in Shamanism was eluding me.

Auriana sat down next to me. She had piercing green eyes, and I soon learned that this was her second trip to Peru. She told me that spiritual growth was not a one-shot deal. That you approached it in stages, dealing with the various levels.

In the middle of our harmless conversation she suddenly looked at me with more intensity.

"What's the matter?" I said, feeling a bit awkward.

"I see something."

"What?"

"I can see that you have been a Shaman before. I can see you as a healer, throughout many incarnations. You are very sensitive, and you have to learn to connect with your own power. This is going to be a very important journey for you."

Auriana spoke with such confidence and strength it took me aback. How had she seen this? What form did this vision take?

Then the trance was broken and it seemed to occur to both of us at the same time that we were in a bar.

"This is wild, isn't it?" Auriana smiled.

"Wild doesn't even come close," I laughed.

"You know what we need here?" Auriana said. "Music. Something we can dance to. Like on the bus."

"I brought some cassettes with me," I said.

Auriana's eyes lit up. "You did?"

"Up in my room. Hold on and I'll get them."

I fetched the tapes and brought them back and Alberto found a large tape player and set it up in the bar. Soon the whole place was rocking to the music of the Pointer Sisters and the whole group was dancing.

I've always loved to dance, and this moment on the mystical coast of Peru, lost in a strange land with strange people, I felt the impulse come back as strong as ever. Dancing was always my only form of self-expression, the only tool by which I got in contact with my deepest self. I trusted it.

And as the music came to an end, arms were flying as we all reached out to hug whoever we could grab in our group. It was a kind of breakthrough for me. Though I am capable of caring deeply and getting close to people in my life, I don't feel comfortable with physical closeness unless there is an emotional bond. But here it was as though we had known each other for many, many lifetimes.

We were exhilarated as we sat down to dinner, and the sharing didn't stop. Forks took the place of loving arms, and the food was shared and passed around the table like a smorgasbord. It was impossible that I had only known these people two days. It was exciting that I was going to be starting this journey with such old, old friends.

We were up and out by seven the next morning to do breathing exercises with don Riccardo. There was some grumbling about the early hour, but Alberto just laughed it off. There would soon be so much electricity, he said, that seven o'clock would seem like sleeping in. As the trip progressed we would be getting up much earlier than this.

The early morning sun shimmered on the bay as we gathered on the grass. Alberto sprinted across the lawn like an agile cat, playfully stalking his prey and pouncing on Vicki, wrestling her to the ground. Her laughter filled the air as don Riccardo attempted to organize us and begin the work of the day.

Alberto and Vicki returned to the group and don Riccardo took us through a series of breathing exercises that would stimulate, open up, and strengthen our energy centers. These energy centers were called "chakras."

"The Chakras are seven major energy centers in the body according to Hindu traditions," Alberto explained. "According to the Inca traditions there are only five, and if you look at other cultures it varies. But I like the concept of seven because there are seven major nerve plexus correlating to physiology."

"The first Chakra is in the sexual organs at the base of the spine and is associated with reproduction, sexuality, and with the preservation of the species. The second is about two fingers down from the belly button and is associated with family, relationships, and the people you are intimately involved with in your life."

I could see Ellie, directly across from me in the circle, trying to locate her second Chakra with her fingers. I did the same. It didn't feel like anything special.

"The third one," Alberto went on. "Is the solar plexus. It relates to your own identity and how you define and present yourself in the world. It is a center that is defined as having a great deal of power. And remember, the Chakras are not stationary. They are like cones of energy that come out from the body, getting larger as they stretch out. The Chakras are the centers where you obtain natural energy. It's where you feed yourself on the energy from nature. It comes into your body and charges you with a bio-magnetic, bio-electric force from nature. It's a very important type of food that we need."

Alberto paused to collect his thoughts. We were all prodding our bodies to locate the Chakra points. There was something vaguely humorous about it, and Alberto smiled.

"The fourth Chakra is the heart Chakra," Alberto said. "But it is not directly over the heart. It is more in the center of the body."

"The fifth Chakra is the throat and it's associated with communication and self-expression. All the Chakras in the body are charging Chakras. They all bring you energy. All of them, that is, except this one. This is a discharging Chakra. Energy comes in and is released through the feet, the head, and the throat."

I sat in the circle and tried to assimilate all I was hearing. A slight panic set in that I would not remember any of this, and that at a critical time later in the journey I would want to summon up this knowledge that came so effortlessly for Alberto and I would draw a blank. It was like being in college again: 'Name the seven Chakras and their functions.' Except this was different from anything I had ever seen in a textbook. I didn't know yet how different. How important.

Alberto went on. "The sixth Chakra is the third eye, which is referred to as the seat of individual consciousness. It's located on the forehead between the eyes and about an inch above the eyebrows. It's related to the pituitary gland. With the awakening of this Chakra they say that the pituitary gland will crystalize."

"Finally, there is the seventh Chakra. It is associated with the pineal gland and is the seat of cosmic consciousness. It is located at the top of the head. With the awakening of this Chakra there is a merging with the cosmos that takes place."

Alberto stopped, took a deep breath, licked his lips. Behind him the sun glistened off the water. "Everything in the Universe spins in a clockwise direction," he said at last. "And so do the Chakras. You can learn to balance your Chakras by spinning them in a clockwise direction. Don Riccardo will demonstrate how this is done."

Don Riccardo rose and demonstrated, but my mind was still on the Chakras themselves. Again, I strained to remember, to "feel" every word that Alberto was saying. I prodded and poked and felt and couldn't come up with anything. Then I backed off. Took it easier, less like a doctor performing a physical. I ran my hands gently along a plane an inch or so from my body. I felt my breath come quick. Yes, I could feel the points of energy! A warmth and tingling in my hand as I came to each energy center. I looked up and focused on don Riccardo and Alberto. This was more than just talk. Strange as it was, it was real. Real.

As part of our early morning ritual, don Riccardo also took us through the breathing exercise called the Little Death. "When people die in the West," he explained. "They gasp for air and breath in, as an attempt to hold onto life. When the Shaman dies, he exhales, and willingly lets go of life. The Little Death is a breathing exercise which is inhaling and holding your lungs full for twelve heartbeats, and then exhaling and holding your lungs empty for eight heartbeats. We will do this five times."

I wiped the beads of perspiration from my forehead. My God, it seemed there were a lot of numbers in Shamanism. How was one every expected to remember all the counts, the beats, the esoteric numerology?

Don Riccardo continued to explain. "As we enter into an altered state of consciousness, through the breathing exercises, we can journey into what the Shaman calls the non-ordinary reality. We, in the West, may call it dreams or fantasy, but to the Shaman, there are many levels of reality. It is within this altered state of consciousness that we can travel into the lower world and connect with our power animals, or *tonals*. This is an energy form that represents itself to us as an animal of power."

Bruce raised his hand in the circle and Alberto acknowledged it. "When don Riccardo talks about power animals," Bruce said. "Is he speaking metaphorically?"

Don Riccardo seemed to know what he was asking, because he did not wait for Alberto's translation. "Absolutely not," he said. "It is important to realize that this is not just a metaphor for a part of ourselves. It is, rather, an energy form that has a life of its own separate from ourselves. We must exercise our power animal every day or it will leave us. But if we use them, they come to help and to heal us. If we can become one with our power animal we may travel as our power animal travels into the spiritual realm. Into the non-ordinary reality."

We all looked at each other nervously, a bit self-consciously, and don Riccardo prepared to take us through the Little Death. We began breathing, and counted. Breathed, and counted. Breathed, and counted. I could feel my whole body slowing down with each breath. In the moments of silence, my body tingled with the inspiration of the fresh morning air.

"Now," Alberto said very softly. "We must learn to exercise our power animal, to do the dance of the *tonal*. The dance of the tonal is a very graceful and beautiful dance. It begins with holding a ball of energy between your hands. This position is called Embracing the Earth. Feel the energy grow and grow and become stronger. Then simply move and flow with it. The movement in some ways resembles T'ai Chi in its animal-like quality. In fact, it's considered the American Indian form of T'ai Chi."

As I began the dance of the *tonal* I could feel the sun beating down on me. It was already getting very warm. I could feel myself moving with the energy, and I felt the heat more and more. I called to my power animal to come to me.

The group around me fades. All I can feel or hear is my own breath and heartbeat. Then suddenly the rhythm jerks. My breathing pattern and movements change. What is this? What am I? I feel great strength surging through my body, and I seem to be moving like a cat. I am the cat! Suddenly stalking through the jungle and walking alongside a river, I hear other animals making sounds. I feel the dampness of the warm jungle air penetrating my body, and the scent of the earth fills my nostrils. I continue along the bank of the river, traveling deeper into the jungle. I am strong. Powerful. My paws grip the earth and nothing in this jungle frightens me.

Suddenly I'm compelled to turn off onto a path leading deeper into the jungle. I feel the cat taking me, I feel myself shift and move with his body. I'm inside him, looking out his eyes. I smell the sweet scent of the jungle flowers. A drum beats in the distance. My agile body pushes away the jungle vines that block my way and flow over my back.

25

The path empties into a clearing and don Riccardo waits there, perched on a tree trunk, beating a drum. I halt. Don Riccardo looks up and motions me closer. I sit on the ground by his feet. He begins to beat his drum once again and I feel the soothing warmth of the earth against my skin. I feel myself drifting into a trance . . . deeper . . . slower . . . to the slow, rhythmic beat of don Riccardo's drum . . .

Then a sudden voice! Alberto's voice, calling me back. I spring onto all fours, follow the path in fast motion back to the river. I begin leaping through the air, taking long and powerful strides.

Then, suddenly, I blinked myself awake and found myself back in the group, back in my own body. Alberto was in front of me, and he was bringing the group meditation to a close. I felt a tremendous sadness at having to come back so soon. As I opened my eyes, I found myself back in the original position of "Embracing the Earth."

CHAPTER FIVE

The group disbanded, ate breakfast, and met a couple of hours later, down by the dock. Two boats were waiting for us, and we were going to go across to an island to visit the giant Candelabra. It was a figure carved in sand on the side of a mountain which was in the shape of a candelabra. But not just your run-of-the-mill carving. The giant Candelabra was three-hundred feet in length and almost ten feet deep. Don Riccardo told us that this figure was a power center, and we would go there to ask for a vision that would later help us to clarify our personal goals and group goals for the journey.

Paracas: Candelabra

I had the chance to sit next to don Riccardo on the boat trip over. He smiled at me, and I couldn't help but notice how kindly his eyes were, squinting in the hot Peruvian sun. As the boat crossed Paracas Bay he put his hand on my shoulder and pointed off into the distance.

"El Candelabro," he said.

"Yes," I said. "I can see it. It's very large. *Muy grande.*"

"*Si,*" don Riccardo nodded. "*Es muy grande.*"

27

Then don Riccardo proceeded to talk with great energy in Spanish, motioning with his hands. I didn't understand a word he said, but the meaning came through loud and clear. The giant Candelabra spanned from heaven to earth. He looked at me to see if I understood. I nodded, and don Riccardo gently smiled.

As we drew closer to the giant Candelabra I began to get uneasy. The sea was choppy, and I could see no place for the boats to dock. Don Riccardo motioned that he and I should try to wrap our extra clothes in a plastic bag. I looked puzzled, but then it became all too clear. The reason I could see no place for the boat to dock was because there was no place for the boat to dock. We had to moor offshore and climb out of the boat and make our way through the sea to the rocky shore.

As I plunged into the frothy sea I couldn't help but be amazed. This was so different from my life back home. I thought of my mother and my friends and what they would think of this.

I fought my way to shore and turned around to see Carole and Ellie not far behind. Carole was huffing and puffing and moaning and laughing all at the same time. Here she was, approaching fifty, and going through this. As she splattered up to shore she gave me a wild look and a huge grin broke across her face.

"If this doesn't make me tall and thin," she yelled. "I'm going to settle for fat and dumpy!"

"Maybe you should settle for just thin." I said.

We lined up at the base of the giant Candelabra. It was immense. Awe-inspiring. I tried to keep my mouth from drifting open. Who in the world had done this, and why?

Don Riccardo was the first one to make it up to the base of the Candelabra. He stopped halfway up, turned to the group, and began to chant. One by one we walked up the center of the Candelabra. Don Riccardo stood there, gently chanting, and he steered us as we approached him to go either to the left or right of the giant figure.

Several people went before me, and I felt my heart racing. I still had the feel of the sea in my body, and the sun was hot and intense. When it came my turn it was a struggle to climb. The hill was deceptively steep, and I had to dig my heels deep into the sand to make progress. When I drew near to don Riccardo he motioned me right, and I saw for the first time that we were forming a giant eagle, with the wings extending out and away from the center line. I stood in my spot and caught my breath as the last of our group made the grueling trek up.

Behind me I could hear Ellie moaning and groaning. She wasn't prepared, physically, for this trip, and when Ellie is having a tough time she loses her sense of humor completely. It was bad, because Ellie had the additional responsibility of being spirit guide for the day. Two people from the group were chosen each day to be the spirit guides. This meant that we were responsible for the spirit of the group. The spirit guide steps into the role of acting Shaman and looks after the community. A tremendous amount of energy comes through the person who takes on this traditional role. Whatever difficulties the group encounters, the spirit guides are to be there to shoulder the burden, to help, and to take on the difficulty as their own.

When we were all in place a silence enveloped us. I couldn't tell whether it was actual silence, or whether my meditative, trance-like state only made it seem so. Then, shockingly loud and strong against the silence, Alberto shouted out. "Come to us, oh great serpent," he cried out. "Come to us and cleanse us and help prepare us for our death!"

I let myself drift in the trance . . . I could almost see it . . . the serpent as it snaked towards us . . .

"Come to us, oh jaguar of the West!" Alberto cried. "Come to us oh rainbow jaguar with your hind legs in the physical and your front legs in the spiritual! Let us look into the mouth of the jaguar and come face to face with our death!"

One by one he called them, and one by one they appeared in my mind's eye. The jaguar, whose mouth opened as a cave filled with men who chanted around a fire. The eagle, who swooped to carry me to a faraway pyramid. And finally, the horse. It made its way towards me, strong and sturdy. So it was all there. The jaguar for its bravery, agility, and aggressiveness. The eagle for its freedom to soar. And the horse for sure-footedness along difficult ways. This was the vision of my journey. These were the goals I needed to reach.

After the meditation, Alberto instructed us to walk further up the Candelabra and find a spot that felt comfortable. We would continue our meditations privately there. I climbed very, very high, almost to the top of the hill. The mountain was quite steep, and as I looked down the difference between the clear blue sky and the clear blue water almost didn't exist. It gave me the oddest sensation of floating . . . the island was not a part of the earth or sea, but of the sky.

I began to do the dance of the *tonal*, calling upon the horse. Perhaps the height scared me more than I knew, and I was calling upon something with the sure-footedness to extricate me from the dilemma.

Then I saw him approaching . . .

Out of the distant sky he came, thundering, hoofs flashing with great strength and forcefulness. I felt my breath come short as the mighty horse drew nearer and nearer.

Then he was right upon me! But he didn't stop! He continued to plow forward, pushing me away with its fevered nose, and I felt my spirit tumble up, over, and begin to hurtle down through the emptiness of space.

I was going to die! I felt it! The ground rushing up, my frail body crushing into it with tremendous force, splattered like some animal in the highway. But then a lightness! I'm not falling anymore. In fact, I'm riding. And I clear my eyes to see that the great Eagle of the east has swooped down below me and I am riding the soft, downy wings. The Eagle lifts me higher and higher and below I see the Candelabra, growing smaller in the distance, and all the rest of my group, doing their small, tiny meditations on the sand below.

I thank God for the Eagle. How could it have known that I was falling, that I needed it so badly? In the midst of my reveries, I suddenly notice something. The feathery wings are no longer below me. The neck is no longer there for me to grab onto. The Eagle is gone! And yet I fly! I am the Eagle!

For ten minutes I revel in the flight, the freedom, the graceful soaring above all earthly things and concerns. I go out to sea, then back, and eventually circle directly above my physical body meditating on the Candelabra. I look lonely down there. My body needs my spirit. So I flutter down, settle into the flesh-and-blood house my spirit has been assigned to, and once again feel the sand beneath my feet.

At the bottom of the Candelabra we all got together in a group and talked about our individual experiences up on the mountain. It seemed that many had had a vision as vivid and clear as I had. Don Riccardo nodded. It was the place. It was, as he said, a very powerful energy center.

As we made our way toward the boat for the return trip, Carole came up close and joined me.

"I don't know," she said. "Everyone was having such clear visions. Mine weren't that clear at all. In fact, I don't think I even had one. Everybody here is so much more experienced in this sort of thing."

"You may be right," I said. "But this isn't like a job. The experience will come to you as you let it happen."

"You might be right," she said. We walked in silence a ways, then she gave me a funny sidelong look. "Come on," she said. "Tell me. I am a little taller and thinner, aren't I?"

I laughed and we continued back down towards the boats.

CHAPTER SIX

When I awoke at six in the morning I had to lay for a bit to orient myself. Where was I? Who was I? Then a bird chirping outside my window solved the mystery. I was in Nasca, a long bus ride from the giant Candelabra, and I was sleeping in a beautiful hacienda surrounded by flowers and gardens and lush foliage.

Nasca was the home of the power animals. Or so the Shamans believed. At 7:30 we were on our way to the airport to take a flight over the Nasca Plains. It is only from the air that one can see the gigantic figures of birds, fish, and reptiles carved into the desert floor. Some of the carvings were miles long. Nobody knows how they came to be, but the Shamans believe they were created by an ancient Indian civilization as a gift to the Gods.

The flight was breathtaking. The planes were small (holding only six people each), and the flight lasted only a half-hour, but I sat at the window, amazed. The animals carved below were clearly visible. A bird, a dog, a monkey, a fish. I could even see a figure etched into the side of a mountain. It was, I found out later, called the astronaut, and that's exactly what it looked like. It was a human form with a rounded head. The plane swirled and dove and circled the figures far below, and I felt my heartbeat quicken. Our plan was to return to the Nasca Plains in the evening for a ritual to call upon the serpent for our own cleansing and purification.

As the plane landed I felt in dire need of cleansing and purification. My stomach was a little rocky, and I was somewhat dazed from lack of sleep. I ordered a light breakfast and went back to my room to rest. The pace was quickening, and it was beginning to take its toll.

Later that afternoon Professor Lancho, an expert on the Nasca Lines, came to the hacienda to give a lecture. The lines, he said, were over 1,500 years old. There was very little wind or rain in this part of Peru, so they had stayed relatively intact all this time. Now, no one is allowed to walk on the Plains, so the lines remain undisturbed.

Someone asked if they might have been ancient landing spots for extra-terrestrials. Professor Lancho smiled.

"No. Although that has been a fanciful notion, and one that has been much written about, it is not true. Maria Reiche, a German mathematician has developed a theory that the lines are part of an astronomical calendar. Many of the figures are perfectly aligned with the rising and setting of the sun during the solstices." As the lecture began to wind down, Professor Lancho turned around and picked up a small black case that he had brought with him. We all leaned forward curiously.

Nazca: The Hummingbird

"As one final thing," he said. "I want to show you something you have probably never seen before. I want to make it a gift to my good friends, don Riccardo and Alberto."

Professor Lancho reached into the case and gently withdrew a severed human arm. I gasped. My body recoiled, and all around me I could hear moans and sudden intakes of breath.

"This is the mummified arm of a high priestess from an ancient Indian tribe." Professor Lancho proudly told our stunned group. The arm was passed around. We each felt the smooth skin of the mummy's arm. It came to me and I passed it on quickly. After the group's inspection, Professor Lancho ceremoniously presented the arm to Alberto. Alberto thanked him, stared at the arm, and did a miserable job of trying to disguise his utter bewilderment.

We had some free time after the lecture to rest, eat lunch, and lie in the sun. The waxy, mummified arm had taken some of the punch out of my appetite, but by this time I was learning to adjust to any and everything in Peru.

Later in the afternoon we reconvened beneath a shady tree and watched as don Riccardo elaborately arranged crystals, rocks, and shells on an old red cloth. That completed, don Riccardo pulled out several long, beautifully carved wooden staffs and stuck them in the ground in front of the cloth.

We all watched in silence, and then Alberto came from the hacienda and crouched down at don Riccardo's side.

"He is laying out his *mesa*," Alberto explained.

"His table?" Bruce said.

"Well, yes," Alberto went on. "In Spanish *mesa* means table. But it also means plateau. It's a place where the Shamans come to meet the spirits. Don Riccardo found this red cloth in the ruins of an ancient Incan temple. On top of this cloth he places his power objects. These objects have been handed down from generation to generation by various Shaman. They can be used for diagnosis and healing work, and also to help his students to obtain the kind of power and knowledge they need to open up spiritually."

"Is there a specific order to what he's doing?" one of the group asked.

"Absolutely," Alberto nodded. "The mesa is divided into three areas. Three fields. The field of darkness is to the left. The field of light is to the right. The neutral field is in the center, the place of balance between the light and the dark. It is a field for the bringing together of earthly and heavenly energies."

The same person raised his hand. "Does the dark mean bad and the light signify good?"

Alberto shook his head. "Not necessarily. You see, these forces are neither positive nor negative, but it's what we do with them that makes them good or bad."

Don Riccardo cleared his throat and began to speak himself. I sensed more and more that he understood what was happening, what was being said, and that he used his linguistic problems as an intelligent shield behind which to protect himself while initiating us. The two large conch shells on either side of the cloth, he said, were like antennae to receive the energy of the cosmos.

"Don Riccardo," Ralph called out. "What are some of the specific purposes of the power objects? Do they each do something special?"

"There are a total of thirteen power staffs and swords before the *mesa*," don Riccardo said.

I shut my eyes. More numbers. Don Riccardo went on about the various functions of his power symbols. They covered a great range of esoteric functions, ranging from the hound dog to find lost people, to the swordfish which helps find lost mariners. It was so specific that I felt the need to speak up myself.

"Alberto," I said. "Do other Shamans work this way, with these same symbols?"

"The meaning of the symbols will vary from culture to culture," Alberto said. "But the Shaman's *mesa* can be found in one form or another among all native healers. These rituals primarily serve as a reminder that the forces of both nature and the human psyche can be worked with when represented as symbols and objects of power."

Then Alberto rose, stretched his legs. "Tonight we will perform a very unusual ritual. Each of you will be called up to the *mesa* and given a seashell containing a mixture. Don Riccardo has created this mixture himself. You will tilt your head back, hold the shell to your nose, and drink the mixture through your nostril."

Our group was silent. Drink through our nostrils? I flashed a glance to Carole. I must not have heard correctly, but I could tell by the worried look on her face that my ears hadn't deceived me.

"You do not inhale it," Alberto continued. "You swallow as you pour it down your nose. It's kind of like eating a raw oyster through your nose."

Alberto looked out at our sea of silent, anxious faces, and a grin tugged at the corners of his mouth. "It's not so bad," he said. "Really. This will be followed by a mixture made from the San Pedro cactus. It is similar to many used by North American Indian Shaman in their Shamanic rituals. This drink has a drug-like quality to it, and when used in a sacred way within the ritual, will keep us all connected to don Riccardo."

I felt my heart begin to sink. This had not been in the brochure back in Long Island. I had never taken drugs in my life. Never. Even as a teenager when my friends were experimenting with marijuana, I always declined. I always had a gut feeling that drugs would inhibit spiritual growth, that they slowed down the journey towards enlightenment rather than accelerated it.

While lost in these concerns Alberto went on to say that in preparation for the rituals of the evening we were to do the Tarot. We were to choose one card that we felt was "our" card. I knew about as much of the Tarot as I did about drugs, but when I looked down at the deck that he arranged face down in a circle on the ground, it seemed as though one card stood out from the rest. It was brighter, luminous. I turned the card over. It was the Empress, sitting on a throne, surrounded by birds. My ignorance of the Tarot actually helped in my interpretation, and I let myself go into a meditation.

The Empress was telling me something . . . she was telling me to embrace my power, to accept that position and be able to see myself in that light. It was a gentle card, a nurturing image, but extremely powerful at the same time. I sensed that the message was clear, direct, and pure. I was to seek out that power, to seek out the Empress within me. To nurture her, and to let her grow.

We left the hotel at 8:45 that evening, incongruously bundled up for what was to be a chilly evening. The contradictions of the trip were everywhere, even in the weather. Bathing suit in the day, North to the Yukon gear in the evening.

But nobody laughed or joked. This was a serious matter. Perhaps others in the group were thinking about what lay ahead. The mixtures that we were to drink through our noses, and the drug-like state we were going to be put under.

When the bus stopped and we silently got out at the Nasca Plains, the moon was full and very bright. I didn't need the small flashlight I'd brought along. There wasn't a sound in the whole world. Then Alberto stood before us and translated as don Riccardo spoke.

"Tonight don Riccardo is going to take you into the world of the *naqual*," Alberto said. "This is the world of the spiritual, the world of the formless. The ritual involves calling upon the spirit of the south, the serpent. What you will experience tonight is the first part of the Shaman's initiation. We cleanse ourselves and are relinquished from past life karma. We must prepare for a spiritual death. Only then is rebirth possible."

Alberto turned and held an open palm at the figure in sand before us. "This figure is called the Needle and Thread. It is a thousand years old and almost a half-mile long. About a third of the way up on the needle is a large double spiral, after which seven turns begin the final zig-zagging to the top of the needle. Each of these turns represents one of the Chakras."

Don Riccardo then quit speaking and set down his *mesa* not far from the spiral, facing east, where the tip of the needle pointed. All of us were to put our own particular power objects onto the *mesa* for energizing. I had worn a crystal pendant. I put it on the red cloth and we all formed a circle and sat watching don Riccardo. We were warned not to leave the circle without one of his power objects. For this ritual we needed to keep connected to him.

Don Riccardo prepared the mixture, flanked by his two chosen assistants, Diego and Auriana. Then it was time. The moment I had been both dreading and excitedly anticipating since the afternoon.

The mixture we were to drink through our noses was a kind of tobacco juice. This increased my nervousness, since I had always had a powerful aversion to tobacco -- an aversion so strong it was almost allergic. The sweet oil used in the mixture was another touch of irony -- Taboo perfume. My mother used to drench herself in Taboo, and I remember as a child smelling the scent long after she had left for the evening. It lingered in the house. Clung to me. I had grown to dislike the scent immensely. And now here I was, ready to drink it down my nose. Was I really going to do this?

Thank God I was not the first in line, because I found myself strengthened by watching those before me go through the ritual and come back to their places in the circle intact. Although it was obviously unpleasant, they had survived. Even Carole, who went before me, took it like a true warrior.

"It's not so bad," she said, settling down next to me, blinking the tears from her eyes. "Don't worry."

Don Riccardo's Mesa

Finally it was my turn. I walked up and took the shell from Diego. My heart was going like crazy in my chest, and I almost couldn't do it. The tobacco, the Taboo . . .

"Do it quickly," Diego said. "It will be less painful."

I did it. Without thinking, without hesitating, I did it. I swallowed as fast as I could, felt it burning a scorching trail down my throat and into my stomach. As soon as I drank it I thought I was going to pass out and I felt my legs start to go out from under me. I felt Diego's hands cupping my arms. I could barely stand, felt dizzy, almost fell again.

"Are you okay?" I heard Diego's voice close to my ear. "Are you okay?"

I righted myself and blinked the dizziness away. "I'll be all right," I said, trying my best to sound confident.

I wouldn't say I walked back to my spot in the circle. Crawl would be a better description. And as soon as I sat I felt my body begin to shake. My teeth chattered. I felt out of control. I looked up and down the circle and could find nobody else who was reacting this way.

"I'm scared," I said to Carole.

She put her hand on my arm. "It's okay."

"No. I mean it. Don Riccardo better be the Shaman he's made out to be, because I have no idea what's happening to my body."

I couldn't stop shaking, and I had the sensation that nothing was beneath me. Nothing holding me steady. It was like the Eagle swooping me up during my meditation at the Candelabra, only much scarier.

"Am I on the ground?" I said to Carole.

Carole reached over and took a blanket and covered me. Then she turned and said in a whisper. "Now I know why I'm here."

I just looked at her. "What . . . what do you mean?"

"I mean that I now know why you showed me that brochure in your office last year. You needed someone to guide you, to make sure you got to Peru." She smiled at me, then her voice grew very serious. "You're going to have an incredible experience here. I know it. I feel it."

Then don Riccardo stood, shook free his jet-black, shoulder-length hair, and began to chant. He was calling on the spirits of the Four Winds. He wore a ceremonial robe and walked around our circle, and the vividness of the image snapped me out of my concern for myself. The moonlight on the Plains, the scent of the mixture, the shock to my senses, this crazy pot-bellied Indian with the dazzling hair and hypnotic voice . . . it was an image I would carry with me for the rest of my days. I watched, mesmerized, as he did his work.

Don Riccardo got the attention of the spirits by spitting the perfume, whistling, and lighting a cigar. I was suddenly conscious of Carole laughing softly beside me.

"What is it?" I said.

"I come all the way to Peru to get away from whistling, and here he is, whistling."

I started to laugh myself. "What about me? The tobacco, the perfume . . ."

I shook my head at the irony of it. The things that were most intrusive in our lives back home were the very essence of the ritual thousands of miles away.

But my amusement was short-lived. I felt the scorching, acrid scent of the mixture again in the pit of my stomach, and I knew in an instant that I was going to be sick. Don Riccardo continued his chanting, and I could feel my breath growing shallow, almost to the point of hyperventilating. I called upon don Riccardo to help me, but it was hopeless. I stumbled to his *mesa*, got a power object to protect me in my time away from the circle, and staggered away. Jordon, one of the spirit guides for the night, came with me and stayed with me while I got sick.

When I finished I leaned on Jordon for support and he helped me back to the circle. I was both relieved and embarrassed. Why had this happened to me? Nobody else had gotten sick.

I was still trying to connect with don Riccardo. This was a nausea that was more than pure physical reaction to the tobacco juice. I tried to connect to don Riccardo, to feel and understand his power. I could hear him telling me to breathe deeply and slowly. Each time I would start to gag, and each time don Riccardo would start chanting loudly and shaking his rattle at me, the nausea subsided. Auriana came over to me and said that there was nothing to fear. I was wide open and vulnerable, nothing more. She showed me how to protect myself from the lower level energies that could be attaching themselves to me, by blocking the energy centers with my hands. Fine. I was willing to try anything.

But I was no sooner settling my poor stomach down when don Riccardo's assistants began walking around the circle with a pail of the San Pedro mixture. Don Riccardo had been simmering it for hours all day. I couldn't believe I was going to actually drink this. Not after what I had just been through.

But it was necessary. No, more than necessary. It was critical. The San Pedro mixture was to help us step into the *naqual*, the non-ordinary state of the Shaman. This was the whole reason I had abandoned all that I had safely known in the understandable boundaries of my New York life. I couldn't risk not taking it.

I drank it. It was very bitter, and it was followed by sugar to ease the unpleasantness of the taste. I was still nauseous from the tobacco juice, and the San Pedro mixture went down with no other sensation at the time but one of being bitter.

Little did I know . . .

CHAPTER SEVEN

The sensation began to take hold about ten minutes later. At that time don Riccardo showed us the next part of the ritual, which consisted of walking one at a time into the spiral, and then walking out again. My head felt fuzzy. Fuzzy, but alert and synchronized as it had never been before. So subtle was the change that initially I wasn't consciously aware of anything happening at all. It snuck up on you.

Don Riccardo told us to watch the other members of our group very closely as we did the ritual. "Don't just look at their eyes and heads and hands and legs," he said. "Look beyond that. Look beyond the physical to see the spiritual energy surrounding the actual body. Then you will see the power animal. You will see the animal stalking you."

He was right. My eyes opened wide with amazement. I suppose there was a part of me that was resistant to the notion of power animals stalking one. A small part, but there nevertheless. A last, stubborn holdout from my upbringing and education. But now I could see it. Any vestige of doubt that was lingering from my life in Long Island was gone.

I watched as the people entered the spiral and saw the animals stalking them. Some had birds. Some had bears. Some had wild colors shooting out of the top of their heads. We whispered to each other what we were seeing, and we were seeing the same things.

Then it was my turn. Again, I rose on trembling legs. Billy, the other spirit guide, helped me up, and I moved towards the spiral. I looked back at the group, but they seemed impossibly distant, lost in the vastness of night and moon and Peru.

I entered the spiral and stood at the center for a moment. Some people had rushed through. I wanted to savor the experience. But then it turned different. Odd. I couldn't name it, but it was as though I had become completely disoriented and couldn't hope to find my way out of the spiral.

I told myself to be calm. It couldn't be that difficult. Everybody else had gone in and out and back to the circle. I felt that I was spending too much time in the spiral, that I was somehow holding things up. But I was powerless to move. I shut my eyes and concentrated.

Then, in the distance, I could hear a lot of noise coming from the group. Don Riccardo started shaking his rattle and chanting loudly. He's calling to me, I thought. And I'm really screwing it up. It's like the sound they play on television talk shows to signal a commercial coming up, that the guest is going on and on too much. That was me.

Then, after what seemed an eternity, I began to stumble out of the spiral. I was no clearer about where I was than I was before, but I knew it was imperative that I begin moving. Then Billy appeared before me, his hand held out, and I took it. He escorted me back to the group and I have never, ever, in all my life before or since, been so happy to see a bunch of people.

Nazca: The Needle & Thread

I half-sat, half-fell into my position and kept quiet, trying to assimilate what was happening. Diego came running up to me, excited.

"Do you know what many people saw when you were in the spiral?" he said. I shook my head. "A serpent!" he said. "A huge one. It surrounded your body and came out of your head."

He turned and left, leaving me with this information. I tried to clear the cobwebs. I had had no sense of a serpent around me, but don Riccardo had said we were going to call him. That the serpent would cleanse us.

My nausea came and went, then came again. Don Riccardo treated me for it, chanting loudly and shaking the rattle, and each time he did I felt my nausea dissipate.

The next step in the ritual was to pair off and walk out onto the Needle. Carole and I agreed to be partners. We approached don Riccardo and he gave us a power staff to take out for protection. It was important that we remained connected to him when we were out at the end of the Needle.

Carole and I made our way to the third Chakra of the Needle and meditated, danced the *tonal*, and called to our power animals. They came. Mine were the horse and the serpent. The horse danced with me, the serpent wound in and out of my consciousness. I was deliriously happy, though "happy" is an insufficient word.

Time passed. How much, I don't know. But I suddenly saw don Riccardo walking straight towards us. He came right up to Carole and stared her in the face.

"Are you okay?" he said.

"Yes," Carole said. "I'm fine."

He then turned to me and began to make a strange gesture at my throat. I felt like something was being pulled out. Not physically. Not by sticking his hands through my mouth and down my tonsils. He never touched me. But the sensation was powerfully that of somebody yanking something out of my throat. I started to gasp and gag. It felt so good that I wanted to cry, but the combined sensations of pleasure and gagging made it impossible. When it was through he took my head in his hands and blew on the top of it. An energy swelled within that filled me from the bottom of my feet to the top of my skull. I almost wanted to cry at the nurturing quality of this unusual healing process. Then don Riccardo hugged me. Such a large man, yet so gentle. From that moment on I trusted don Riccardo implicitly. He was someone who would never let me down. He was what he claimed to be.

As we walked back to the circle I noticed don Riccardo moved close to a Spanish-speaking woman in our group, Lourdes, and had a few words with her. She nodded, and he continued on his way.

Lourdes came up to me, walked close by. "Don Riccardo just told me something about you," she said.

"What was it?"

"He said that you haven't been loved in a long time. He also said that not everyone can be as sensitive as you are."

I walked the rest of the way back to the circle in a kind of stupor. I thought of my long-ago relationship that had ended just about the time I was making my decision to come to Peru. I thought about the year of abstention from the world of men that followed. Don Riccardo had somehow known that about me. And I thought, as I took my place in the circle, that he could see right through the many layers that make up who I am. My trust in the man was complete.

At three o'clock in the morning the ritual ended. All of us gathered our belongings and went back to the bus without a word. All of us were exhausted. Spent. Emptied in a way none of us had ever been before.

Don Riccardo and Alberto were late getting to the bus, and when the Shaman boarded, I could tell something was wrong. He was weaving from side to side, almost like a drunk, and his pallor had grown pale and wan. Suddenly he looked unconscious, and we realized don Riccardo was very sick.

Alberto was the first to realize the gravity of the problem, and he sprang into action. I don't know what I expected, but it wasn't what I saw. I had been far too accustomed to people screaming for a doctor, for ambulances, for syringes and medicines. But Alberto knew what to do. He grabbed a bottle of water and began a Shamanic healing technique of sucking the illness out of don Riccardo, using the water as a medium. For fifteen minutes or longer this went on; Alberto taking a mouthful of water and frantically sucking at the chakra points of don Riccardo. Then Alberto violently spit the water out the window of the bus, pushing himself beyond endurance, beyond the point of exhaustion. We all watched in utter silence, stilled before the incomprehensible scene enacted before us.

It was only later that we learned what had happened. Don Riccardo, after the rest of us had begun to filter back to the bus, had gone to a private spot to bury the mummified arm that had been presented to him earlier that day. The arm had belonged to a priestess who held great resentment towards men, for it had been men who had raped and pillaged her country. A spirit woman, the priestess herself, had given him and some of the others this information during the ritual.

That was what had made him sick. He had absorbed all the pain and fury of the priestess, and of the lost civilization that symbolized her muted anger. The arm had to be returned to the earth, and when it was, the negative karma associated with the lost civilization was buried with it. Alberto said that as a result thousands more people all over the world would be free to follow the path of the Shaman.

What an end to the night . . .

CHAPTER EIGHT

The next morning dawned bright and warm. We had all slept in, due to the lateness of the ritual the night before, and most of my nausea was gone.

I hardly had time to ruminate about the experiences of the previous night when I suddenly heard a woman screaming. It was Auriana. I ran to where she lay on the ground, with don Riccardo close by doing a healing on her. Nicole was standing there, looking concerned. As I was about to run past her, she put out her hand to stop me. She was a powerful member of this tribe and I was not about to challenge her.

"Don't get any closer," she said. "Keep back."

"What's going on?" I asked.

"Auriana is still feeling the pain from the ritual last night," Nicole said, never once taking her eyes from the healing. "She had taken on the physical pain of the high priestess and was experiencing a stabbing in her shoulder, just as the high priestess had when her arm was cut off."

I watched, completely stunned. Could this really be happening? Auriana was screaming in agony. Then, just as suddenly, she went limp. She started to cry. It was over. We moved close and tried to comfort her and she told us of how the high priestess had spoken through her. The high priestess didn't trust men . . . didn't trust don Riccardo. I crouched and watched Auriana, weak and drenched with tears. My own disbelief had vanished.

Don Riccardo was out on the grass, and one by one we went out to sit with him. Someone in the group asked about numerology. Don Riccardo nodded, and explained that based on your birthdate, there was a way to figure out the number that was associated with you. It was a long, complicated scheme and I couldn't follow the steps that don Riccardo was going through. At any rate, my number turned out to be seven.

"It is good," he said. "Seven is the color of purple, and purple is a very spiritual color. The symbol for this number is the Empress."

I thought of the tarot card I had chosen. The Empress. Coincidence? Or just another in the growing series of synchronistic events here in the Peruvian wilderness?

We were suddenly called to the dining room for a late brunch. While gathered around the table, we talked about the ritual of the night before. What was amazing to me was how similar people's experiences were, and how so many people had seen the exact same thing.

"Like you," Alberto said, looking directly at me. "I saw a serpent surrounding your body last night, Irene."

"You did?" I said, startled.

"Absolutely."

"I didn't see or feel it, Alberto," I said. "But I know I was terribly disoriented."

"It is the nature of the serpent," Alberto said. "A serpent winds and weaves and circles back over and through itself. It not only cleanses, but disorients as well. You were lost until don Riccardo called the serpent back into the ground."

"What if he hadn't?" I said.

Alberto just smiled. "That's why we took the Shaman to the Plains of Nasca."

The bus ride back to Lima was over eight hours long. It gave me a lot of time to think about quelling my nausea, and to mull over the events of recent days.

Already, the trip had justified the suspicions I'd had about my self and world for many, many years. But I was helpless to define it. I was still too much locked up into the parceling-out world of psychoanalytic theory, "problem-solving," and dealing with everything in a brittle, cause-and-effect way. My experiences were bizarre enough that in another place and time one would be inclined to write them off to various understandable phenomena. So, you say you've experienced a serpent around your body? Uh huh. Tell me, what did you ingest that night? Tobacco juice and perfume and the juices of Peruvian cactus. Ah hah. Okay. Next.

But it wasn't as simple as that. It wasn't because my subjective experience was shared objectively with other people in the group. They had seen the serpent, too! That fact alone kept one from analyzing what had happened to me in pathological terms. The rules of the game were entirely different.

The only way I could explain it to myself was to think in terms of Carl Jung's work. He talks about a collective unconscious which we all share. It made sense to me that perhaps by entering a state of altered consciousness, we could journey into this collective unconscious. It is only in that arena do we come face to face with our primordial existence. But it was possible to think your way into oblivion. The eight hours on the bus gave me just that chance. Finally I backed off. Relaxed. From this point on I was just going to experience.

I kept my nausea well in check, but as soon as we pulled up before the hotel in Lima I literally ran from the bus to the bathroom. It was impossible that a human being could vomit this much. Throughout my ordeal the group encouraged me. Not at toilet-side, mind you, but close enough. And the gist of their encouragement was that I was really being cleansed. I nodded weary acknowledgement. If this was cleansing, I'd had enough.

We were up again at 4:15 a.m. so we could be sure of catching our early flight to Cuzco. The bizarre hour was imperative, Alberto told us, because in the afternoon the fog rolls over Cuzco and its 11,000 foot elevation, making landing an airplane virtually impossible. What next, I thought. What next?

Cuzco

What next was a very strange and powerful healing. Shortly before the plane took off, Madison -- a well-known psychic healer -- came up behind me and worked on my torso for a moment. The nausea was suddenly gone. Completely, utterly gone.

"What did you do?" I asked, amazed.

"Your chakras were spinning in the wrong direction," she answered matter-of-factly. "It was probably the tobacco juice you drank the other night that got them spinning erratically."

And that was that. Chakras? Energies spinning in wrong directions? My God, how far I was from Long Island! As we got on the plane don Riccardo came and sat next to me. He was concerned at the intensity and duration of my sickness. It seemed we both wanted to talk to each other very badly, but the language barrier was simply too great. So we sat in silence while the plane soared over the incomprehensible land of Peru. Sat, and watched, and immersed ourselves into the exquisitely comfortable silence.

I thought I was out of the woods, but when we landed in Cuzco I had to think again. This time it was the altitude. On a map, 11,000 feet seemed so innocuous. Digits and numbers on a piece of paper. But the oxygen reality of the height rendered almost incapable of moving. Somehow I fumbled my way to the bus and we were off again.

Cuzco was a pleasant change from the urban brown of Lima. It was quaint, cobblestoned, and colorful. The air -- what there was of it -- was sweet and clear. Our hotel, Los Marqueses, was in the middle of a long, narrow street. I struggled up the stairs, found a bed that had my name written all over it, and collapsed.

Later we took a bus to Tambo Machay, the ruins of an ancient Incan temple, that was situated even higher than Cuzco. We chewed on coca leaves to fight the effect of the altitude.

We were going to Tambo Machay to find the path we needed to follow during this leg of the journey. We had experienced the south, had called upon the serpent. Now we were calling on the wind of the East, the eagle, and the West, the jaguar, to help us die. It was not a literal death, of course. No, it was a death far more important than that. It was a putting to rest of the selves we had been in the past. This was a death that would lead us to a spiritual and eternal rebirth.

Tambo Machay was a colorful place, peopled with enterprising young beggar children who hit us up for money. It was grassy and green and surrounded by beautiful mountains. A far cry from the arid dreariness of Lima.

Breathing exercises at 12,000 feet is different from breathing exercises at sea level. We were all light-headed immediately, but don Riccardo patiently took us through our exercises.

Alberto stood and once again invoked the spirits of the four winds to come to us. He called the serpent of the south, and once again I found him staring me eye to eye.

"Come closer," I said to him. "I invite you to embrace me."

I kept my body from instinctively clenching. I have never liked snakes, yet I felt the serpent surrounding me. This is what the journey is all about. Overcoming the fears of the past, shedding the apprehensions as a snake sheds its skin.

I was immersed in the sensation of the snake when Alberto's voice snapped me back to the present.

"Come to us, oh great Jaguar! The rainbow Jaguar from the West with your hind legs in the physical and your forelegs in the spiritual. Let us walk across your back, oh great Jaguar!"

I felt the presence . . . black, powerful . . . flash across my consciousness.

"Look into the mouth of the Jaguar!" Alberto cried out. "Look into the eyes of death!"

I felt myself slip . . . I saw the Jaguar's face. His mouth opened wide, unbelievably wide, and I felt myself go deep into the darkness of its mouth ...

Tambo Machay

What was I seeing? The brain strained to interpret, but it was all in vain. I saw men and women in white robes, wearing large golden headpieces, facing in one direction as if listening to a speaker.

"Who are you?" I asked. My voice sounded as though I were speaking in an echo chamber. I didn't know if the sound was real or only in my imagination.

"We are the Masters," came a voice in return.

Then the blackness became a cave . . . the entrance to a cave, and a man who looked like a monk greeted me at the opening and led me silently to where there was a group of people seated in a circle around a fire, chanting.

"Oh ma kong," they said over and over and over and over. "Oh ma kong, Oh ma kong. Oh ma kong."

"Come sit with us," the monk finally said. *"Come take your place in the circle."*

I sat, conscious of the orange flames licking the sides of the cave wall. Then, as if from a previous, long-forgotten life, I heard Alberto's voice again.

"Come to us, oh eagle!" he cried. "Come to us, oh eagle of the East. Come to us and help us create a vision!"

I'm not sure how, but suddenly I was out of the dark cave, away from the flickering light and chanting faces, and was instead on the back of the Eagle. It lifted me away; higher and higher, till all of Cuzco lay far below me.

I sensed that this would be the end of it, that we would fly together and gaze down on things as the airplane had done over the Plains of Nasca. But no. Suddenly we were over terrain that looked Egyptian, with Pyramids dotting the landscape. I was on solid ground, and I was met by two men in white who were going to do a healing on me. To open my third eye. They laid me down on a marble slab and I could feel the vibration of my third eye as they began to do their work.

Then I heard Alberto calling the great horse of the north, and the healing process abruptly ended as the horse galloped down to me and swept me up. The horse took me to a place I had been before . . . a crystal cave, filled with the memories of past meditations. I stared into the huge crystal in the middle of the cave and felt myself drift deeper and deeper into a trance, oblivious to all else around me.

Then, pulling me back from that distant place, Alberto brought the meditation to an end and we all returned to the position of "Embracing the Earth." I was silent, still lost in my meditation, still not quite back in ordinary reality. The visions were so clear, so real. When I opened my eyes I felt good and healthy. It was the first time in days I had felt so good.

Alberto then produced the package of Tarot cards. He spread them out, face down, in a circle on the ground. We were instructed to chose one. This would indicate the direction we would go in this phase of the journey. Again, one card shined out brighter than the rest. I turned it over. The Empress.

I went off to find a comfortable spot to meditate. The synchronicity of the Tarot card didn't shock me anymore. I was too used to the marvels of this journey to suspect coincidence. I closed my eyes, and the let the voices come.

"It is time for you to step into your power with grace," the voice said. *It was a woman's voice. Gentle, yet firm. "To step with dignity and compassion. The power is there. You must recognize that which you once knew."*

Suddenly, in the depths of my meditation, it all made perfect sense. Of course! How much simpler could it be? It was all a matter of recognizing what one already knew. And in the depths of this meditation I saw brief flashes of other times, other civilizations, in which I was able to embrace my power and use it for healing others. An Indian medicine woman . . . a healer in ancient Greece . . .

"Step into your power," the voice implored again.

Yes, I thought, tears beginning to crowd my eyes. This woman knows. This woman has touched something deep inside of me. In the depths of my innermost soul I knew she had spoken the truth.

The meditation ended. Contrary to other times, I felt no urgent need to run to the rest of the group and share my insights. No, this was more personal. This was a very private message, and I held it close.

We walked down the mountain to the waterfall which represented the four directions. While don Riccardo chanted we each went to the waterfall, first taking a drink, then rubbing the water on our forehead, heart, and stomach. This completed the cleansing process and prepared us for the next phase of our initiation. To look into the eyes of the Jaguar and to face death. Head on.

CHAPTER NINE

The train from Cuzco to Machu Picchu left very early. I was roused from my bed at five o'clock, and I wondered why it was that everything in Peru had to start at the crack of dawn.

The train was very old and seats cramped, but the view was magnificent. The closely-set rooftops of Cuzco glistened before us in the early morning sun. Snow-capped mountains in the distance seemed to protect and cradle this ancient City of Lights. With the music of El Condor Pasa filling the train, we crept quietly out of the awakening city. We were actually going down in altitude, descending a total of 3,000 feet, and I could feel the change immediately. The energy came back. Breathing was not such an exercise.

But with the climb down also came the renewed presence of Peru's abject poverty. Whole families lived in squalid shacks by the side of the railroad tracks. Dirty, naked children ran amidst piles of garbage. There was a bleakness there, a hopelessness that hurt me to my very soul. Americans are sheltered from such international unpleasantries. It was hard to stare it in the face.

The train stopped now and then, and women would crowd the tracks, plying their alpaca blankets and woven goods. Children peddled grimy packets of fruit and candy. The train moved on, and I shut my eyes. It seemed impossible we were journeying to one of the most spiritual places on the face of the planet. The road to heaven was lined with thorns.

At last I saw the beginnings of the Urubamba River. Green foliage sprouted from the bank, and it tapered up and away to reveal the towering green mountain that held Machu Picchu. I felt a knot in my throat, and I thought once again of how much this trip had seemed like <u>The Wizard of Oz</u> back home. I felt it again. The way Dorothy swallowed hard when first seeing the glistening Emerald City.

At the base of Machu Picchu we transferred to a tram and were driven up the side of a winding mountain road to the ruins of the Inca civilization. I tried not to look at the steep drop just to my right. The driver was fast, but seemed to know what he was doing.

At last the tram stopped and the stone walls of the lost Incan city lay before us. This sanctuary, 8,000 feet above sea level, was protected by a dry moat and high wall. Once the exclusive domain of Incan nobles, priests, and priestesses, the imposing gates were thrown open to any tourist who could make his way to the remote outpost.

I took a moment to survey the city alone. I lost myself in a fantasy. I could see how it must have been those thousands of years ago, bright with color and festivity, the ancient Incans busily going about their lives. My reveries were broken by Alberto, who called us to gather around the Funeral Rock.

"We are not alone here," Alberto said. "There are spirit guardians who protect the ancient ruins of Machu Picchu. We must ask their permission to enter, for we are not entering as tourists. We are entering as Incas ourselves, as Children of the Sun. In order for them to accept us, each one of us must go through a death ritual."

We circled the Funeral Rock, each of the four directions guarded by a member of the group. The rest of the group circled around and started chanting. I froze when they began the chant. It was the exact chant of my vision in the cave.

Machu Picchu: "Funeral Rock"

Don Riccardo rose and began calling on the spirits of the four winds. He was naked from the waist up and one could almost see the energy swirl out from his body. Then, one by one, we climbed upon the Funeral Rock and laid down on our backs as the Incas were laid out at the time of their deaths.

As I touched the Funeral Rock an electric shock went through my body. It felt as if the rock itself was vibrating under me. I closed my eyes and don Riccardo came to me to perform the ritual. He worked over my body, touching each Chakra. He tapped on my Third Eye and blew into my heart Chakra and I felt myself begin to float up and out into space. Then don Riccardo clanged his Tibetan bells and I jolted at the reemergence into my physical body.

When the ritual was complete we came off the rock, walked down the hill, and entered the gate of Machu Picchu. But we were not entering as tourists. We were entering as Incas . . . Children of the Sun.

Don Riccardo led us to an area with a stone called the Inti Huatana. In Quechua Indian language it means "place where the sun is fastened." The stone was huge, and it was carved to look something like a podium reaching towards the sky.

Machu Picchu: Inti Huatana

"There is a legend about this stone," Alberto explained. "It is said that the Incas had a large crystal on top of the rock that was used for telepathic communication, for healing and for building. Hiram Bingham, the first Westerner to discover Machu Picchu in 1911, saw the crystal. But when he returned with others, the crystal was gone. It is believed that the Incas took it and hid it in the mountains where the white man could not steal or use it."

Don Riccardo led us through the ritual. It involved circling the stone and leaning our hands and foreheads against the rock to absorb its power, to absorb its ability to awaken the Third Eye in all of us. I felt it, and backed away, smiling. Non-ordinary reality was becoming almost ordinary, I was so accustomed to it.

Don Riccardo knew everything about Machu Picchu. He walked it as you or I would walk through our living-rooms. He showed us the places that tourists were not remotely aware of. He took us to see the sacred place where auras were read and healings were done. We went to the Temple of the Condor, symbol of strength. Don Riccardo pointed to a passageway at the base of the rock, and encouraged us to crawl into its hidden chambers.

I hesitated, but then went on ahead. The passageway opened into a small and musty chamber. I sat there for a moment, wondering how many souls in this world, through time, had known the inside of this place. I felt the skin prickle on the backs of my hands.

The sun was setting, and we were the last group to leave the ruins. We followed a risky path along the railroad tracks to get back to a small town where we would sleep for the night, our flashlights flickering in the growing darkness. There were holes here and there, and the drops were steep. At one point we had to walk right on the tracks through a tunnel, and I thought of what would happen if a train came along at that instant. But it didn't. Wouldn't. To look at don Riccardo and Alberto, you knew that it couldn't. The trust was implicit. We felt like we were protected.

We arrived at last in the village, dirty and tired but very much alive. We continued straight on to some nearby hot springs, and relieved our aching bodies with a moonlit swim. Some went nude. Others, like me, brought bathing suits. It was getting chilly out, and the warm water felt good. I nestled down into the bubbles and soft ooze and gazed up at the starry sky. Why had it taken me this many years to come to this place? Why hadn't I trusted my long-ago instinct and accelerated this state of evolution, this appreciation of true beauty, not the pre-packaged "beauty" of our consumer-mad society?

Relax, I told myself. Things happen at their own pace. You weren't ready until this moment. Be thankful it happened at all. I leaned back in the warm, bubbling water and smiled at the stars. I'd never been so completely happy in my life.

I should have known it, but it still caught me by surprise. I'm talking about the constant early-morning awakenings. This time it was 4:30, and the knock was emphatic enough to let us know there was no rolling back under the covers. Shamans have crummy hours.

A glass of fruit juice held us till we reached Machu Picchu. We began our hike back along the same set of railroad tracks as we'd traversed the night before. Only now could we all see how dangerous it had been, how deep and unforgiving the drops. This was a definite case of ignorance being bliss.

Alberto had arranged for us to enter Machu Picchu earlier than allowed. He seemed to have free reign to do whatever he wanted there. I heard that it was because one of his groups had once done a healing on the owner of the restaurant at Machu Picchu and brought him out of a coma. Out of gratitude, Alberto is allowed access to Machu Picchu at times when it usually closed to the public.

Machu Picchu: The Pachamama

As we entered the Inca City of Lights, we made our way to the Pachamama. This is a stone twenty feet long and ten feet high. It represents Mother Earth. Yesterday, don Riccardo explained, we had connected with the Sun, and had unleashed the masculine sides of ourselves at the Inti Huatana. Today we would go to the Pachamama and awaken the feminine.

This required a lot of conscious thought, as opposed to the free-form meditation we had been doing up to this point. Each of us took three coca leaves to the base of the Pachamama as an offering. Each leaf represented a wish or goal that we wanted to achieve in relation to our Shamanic initiation.

I put down the leaves and moved to a spot where I could be alone, to really think out my true goals.

My first goal was to step into my power without fear or hesitation. It was my entire purpose for being here. I had always feared that power would alienate me, that if I was competent and confident there would be natural resentment and I would be an outcast of sorts. It is very lonely to have nobody to look up to. I had a tremendous deal of trouble with a very basic concept of human relationships. That the male and female should come together and face each other as equals, without games of leverage or "oneupsmanship."

My second wish was to develop my healing abilities. Spiritual fulfillment was fine and well, but I still had that nagging longing to do something for the greater good, to apply in a practical sense the fruits of my spiritual enlightenment. Enough instances in my life had convinced me that I had latent healing ability. My second wish was to bring it to fruition, to help it realize its full potential.

My third goal was trickier. It had nothing to do with cosmic Gods or windswept power animals. It was far away from the dazzling mysticism of Peru, of don Riccardo doing his wonderfully insane half-naked dance while the incomprehensible stars blazed overhead. No, my third goal was the humdrum, run-of-the-mill wish of a woman from New York who had to live in the 20th Century. It was a wish to come to grips with the problems with my mother.

I've always believed that we choose our parents in order to learn a lesson in this lifetime. No challenge, nothing learned. But she pushed my limits of exasperation to such extremes that I had completely lost sight of what it was that I could possibly be learning from her. It was a story so old I could barely bring myself to dredge it up again. She and I never got along. She and my sister seemed to form a very strong alliance when I was a child. I found myself aligning with my father and the arguments multiplied and I would retreat to my bedroom, feeling the cause and catalyst for most of the familial dissention. My wish was not for happiness or some improbable moment of harmony with my mother. Things are what they are. I only wished for understanding. I only wished to learn the lesson I was meant to learn. I knew that I could not completely embrace my power until I healed that child within.

As I completed my meditation, Alberto called us together and instructed us to form two rows, one of men and the other of women. Don Riccardo began his chant, calling upon the spirit of the Pachamama to help us awaken the feminine part of ourselves to connect with Mother Earth. One by one, alternating men and women, we approached the Pachamama. We put our offerings at the base and then turned and pressed our backs hard against the stone. The ritual itself was a way of putting into concrete action our wishes and goals. It was a way of changing the internal message from "I wish," to "I am."

I completed my ritual, invoking the three desires I held most dear to my heart, and slowly walked away from the stone. I was still feeling the energy in a very powerful way, however, and chose not to watch the others of the group, but instead continue the meditation at another stone in private.

I sat at a point overlooking the mountain. What a strange, exotic land. How far from Long Island. And as I sat in my trance-like state it suddenly occurred to me that was part of the problem. Part of the problem and part of my work. Was this knowledge only reserved for those of us who had the time, money, inclination, and guts to get on a plane out of Miami? No. Doubtless there were many back in Long Island. Women and men who would never find themselves in this position because of one thing or another, who yet wished to be educated about holistic therapy and philosophy. As I sat in my trance-like state I suddenly saw Alberto away from this strange land. I saw Alberto in a very familiar setting. The United States. Long Island. I saw him conducting workshops in the belly of the beast, as it were, to develop spiritual enlightenment close to the lion's den. And I was a major part of it. Arranging it. Making it happen. This was the practical application of my work in this frightening and beautiful faraway land.

I wanted to rush to Alberto's side and communicate this right away, but the timing wasn't right. Alberto was busy dividing our group into two parts. One group would go with him to the top of Huayna Picchu, a brutal climb of over an hour. The rest would remain with don Riccardo at the bottom. Then there would be an attempt at telepathic communication from one group to the next, just as it was practiced in the times of the Incas.

A part of me wanted to gamble and try the climb to the top, but I was assigned -- as the spirit guide for that day -- to remain at the bottom. While Alberto and his group climbed, we at the bottom had a chance to talk with don Riccardo. The language barrier wasn't a great problem, and I found myself grateful that I was able to spend my time this way and not tormenting my slightly out-of-shape Long Island body on the brutal slopes of Huayna Picchu.

While waiting, we sat in a circle and spoke with don Riccardo in our broken Spanish. I spent some time with Sadie. We were a close and warm group. Except, that is, for Carole. It seemed that everyone else was finding their own specialty except for her. Carole followed the group from ritual to ritual, and she always gave the impression of being on the outside looking in. An observer, watching the others while remaining out of touch with what she, herself, should be learning from the experience.

When Alberto and his group were nearing the top, Sadie said she felt the powers of Machu Picchu working on her, and that she felt she could "tune in" to us as never before by reading our palms. One by one we gathered around and she illuminated aspects of our pasts that had us all open-mouthed. Then she turned to Carole.

"Your turn," Sadie smiled.

Even though Carole was fond of calling herself the "spiritual retard" of the group, there was no disguising her enthusiasm for the "tuning-in" Sadie was about to initiate.

Machu Picchu: Huayna Picchu

Carole sat next to Sadie and stretched out her hands. Within moments, the gleeful anxiousness to have her palms read turned dark. Carole looked upset. Then, like a river overflowing its banks, Carole began to cry hysterically. As Carole told me later, Sadie seemed to induce an immediate vision of one of Carole's traumatic past lives. Carole saw herself as a five-year-old child, running, with bombs going off all around her.

The sobbing continued so desperately that I turned to get don Riccardo. But he had already heard the commotion and was on his way. He took Carole and began doing a healing on her. She sobbed and sobbed and sobbed.

At one point during the healing, several members of the group observed don Riccardo pulling what looked like black thread from her throat. He said that black magic had been used on Carole and that through his healing, he released her from the effect of it. This was the beginning of a releasing and cleansing process for Carole that lasted for days. It had been neither one of our destinies to climb up Huayna Picchu.

When Alberto's group reached the top they looked like nothing more than pinpricks against the lush green. I closed my eyes and meditated and saw a golden eagle with its wings fully spread on the top of the mountain. I mentioned this to don Riccardo and he nodded his head.

"Yes," he said. "The eagle is there."

CHAPTER TEN

I woke early the next morning in the hotel room back at Cuzco. I was tired and hungry and realized that I'd only had one small meal the day before. Sleeping and eating had become low priority items on this trip. Back home I'd be worried to death, feeling like this. I thought that maybe the whole point was to break down my resistance.

Ellie was suffering from severe mosquito bites, which was odd because nobody else was so afflicted. Wouldn't you know. Carole was also sick. At least, that's how we in the West would describe it. If you have this and this and this symptom, then you are sick. The Shaman would say that her present state of disharmony is positive because it is giving her an opportunity to change and reevaluate her life, that it is snapping her out of the cultural trance she lives in. Small comfort now, though, as she lay squirming on the bed. I'd save my Shamanic insight for later. Right now all she was evaluating was the distance to the bathroom.

I dressed and went down to breakfast, hearing Carole behind me moaning about the fact that she had to be sick on the one day we had time to do some shopping. Shopping was Carole's passion in life, the thing that made her tick, the engine that made her run. I thought it strangely significant that she should be denied this one thing on the journey of initiation.

Ellie was already down at the breakfast table, finishing up and preparing for a day of shopping herself. Carole may have loved to shop, but Ellie had it down to a deadly and precise science. Alberto shook his head at her uncommon ability in this area, and suggested that perhaps Ellie alone had changed the economic status of Cuzco.

I did some shopping with a few friends and got back to the hotel fairly early. Carole was still stretched out in bed, going through hell. She looked like death warmed over.

"The water just keeps pouring out of me," she said weakly. "I never knew the human body could hold so much water."

I sat on the edge of the bed and put my hand on hers. "Do you feel well enough to come with us to the Sacsayhuman ruins this afternoon?"

"The what?"

"It's to prepare us for tonight's ritual," I said. "We're meeting in about a half an hour."

Carole just shook her head and laughed. "You've got to be kidding. I can't even drag my body out of bed. There's no way I can go with you this afternoon."

"You're probably right," I said. "It's better for you to rest up now, because you <u>have</u> to come back there with us tonight for the ritual."

Carole just looked at me. "You're not serious?"

"Carole," I said imploringly. "You must come with us tonight. My God, tonight we call upon the spirits of the jaguar and the eagle. This is where we face our death! This is what we've been preparing for!"

"I'm facing my death right here in this hotel room!" Carole shouted, starting to laugh. "I'll manage the dying part of it just fine, don't worry."

I smiled, but deep down I was deadly serious. "This isn't just another vacation, Carole. This isn't the Bahamas with your bathing suit and drinks at poolside. This is important. Think of the whistling. Think of all the things that brought you to this place. This is a cleansing, can't you see that? And you are not being cleansed so you can plead weakness and spend the day sitting in bed reading a book and feeling sorry for yourself. You've got to fight this. This is your preparation."

Carole quit smiling and turned away from me. I sensed she agreed, but didn't want to face it. If I was learning nothing else from this trip, it was that one should not give in to weakness or illness. There's a point to everything.

That afternoon, Alberto and don Riccardo took us to the Sacsayhuman ruins and explained that this was going to be the site of our ritual that night. It was a place where Shamans had come for centuries for their initiation.

"This is the home of the Masters," Alberto explained. "The spiritual beings who come to initiate us, come to help us die and enter into the world of the spirit, of the *naqual*. To the naked eye, the ruins look like just another mountain in Peru, but to the eye of the Shaman, it's a powerful initiation center. There are two caves here, and both will be used in the process."

Alberto turned and led us to the Cave of the Monkeys. "This is where we will come later in the evening to look into the eyes of the Jaguar and ask for the spirit to let us die."

Then Alberto led us over a mountain of rock, down the other side, and into another cave called the Cave of the Light. It was tough climbing, and I wondered how in the world we were going to manage it in the pitch black of night.

As we entered the Cave of the Light, Alberto showed us there was a serpent carved into the wall of the cave. We each ran our hand along the body of the serpent and then proceeded toward the back of the cave, passing through the various chambers. Far in the back we would call upon the spirits of the East. We would call upon the spirits for enlightenment and vision.

We spent an hour or so preparing the cave for our ritual. This meant removing all the debris of modern civilization -- wrappers, bits of glass, and so on -- so that the caves would be free of any substance that wasn't natural to the environment. At the end of it I sat down and smiled. The only woman from Long Island who has ever given a sacred Peruvian cave a bath.

Sacsayhuman

Finally we gathered outside the cave and formed a circle around Alberto. "We will come back here this evening," he said, "to complete our work with the spirits of the East and West. We will sit in a circle tonight, just as we are now. Don Riccardo will call upon the spirits of the four winds. As I feel your readiness for the initiation process, I will come and take you by the hand, one by one, and lead you to the Cave of the Monkeys. As you enter, there will be a guardian of the cave in the first chamber, but you are to walk all the way to the back and sit in the last chamber with your legs in a half-lotus position. You will remain there, meditating for three minutes. During these three minutes you will call upon the spirits of the West and look into the eyes of the Jaguar. This is where you ask for your death. It is important that you come to this ritual completely prepared, realizing exactly what it is you are giving up, and what it is you want to gain. When your three minutes are up I will come for you so that another may begin the process. As we make our way to the Cave of the Light, we will be stopped by a spirit guide who will block our way. You will be asked, 'Why do you wish to pass? What is your purpose?' And you must state your purpose. If you are truly prepared to meet your death and your response rings true from the heart, then you will be allowed to enter the Cave of the Light."

Alberto briefly paused and surveyed our silent, serious faces. We knew this was important, and all of us were hanging on his every word.

"As you enter the Cave of Light," Alberto continued. "Run your hand along the body of the serpent and you will see a guardian of the cave in the first chamber. Continue to the back of the cave and, again, sit in a half lotus position for three minutes."

Someone raised a hand and Alberto acknowledged it.

"Three minutes is a short time," the man said. "What if nothing happens?"

"Many people have had powerful experiences in those three minutes," Alberto said. "And if it doesn't happen in that amount of time, then it's not going to happen. This is why it is so critical to come to this ritual prepared."

Alberto went on to explain that we were to bring an offering to the spirits. We, after all, were going to be given something significant from the spirits. We should leave something significant in return. I thought about it a moment. I remembered a small crystal I had brought with me that had been given to me by a friend. I liked the energy of this crystal, and it was small enough to carry around. It was the only thing I'd brought with me that seemed special. That would be my offering to the spirits.

That afternoon we did the Tarot again. It was sort of like fine-tuning the spiritual senses in preparation for the events of the night. Alberto and don Riccardo again talked about the importance of being prepared ahead of time for the ritual. After the selection of our Tarot card, we were instructed to choose another partner within the group. My card was the Empress, of course, and I went off to find a partner. At first I fastened on Nicole, but she shook her head. It didn't feel right. Then my eyes fell on Madison, and she and I went back to her hotel room. She turned over her card. The Emperor! A perfect match!

I took a deep breath and stared into the card. The message was clear. The Emperor told me that both he and the Empress were very powerful, but their power is different. Each can accept and respect the power of the other without feeling threatened or in competition. "Step into your power," the card told me. "You won't be rejected or considered a threat. Someone who is your equal and counterpart will admire your power and respect you for it." I had chosen my partner well.

I gave the card back to Madison, stood, and went to the hotel window. This was it. The final hour. It was time for me to jettison all the psychoanalytic baggage, the nagging fears, the hesitation that had kept me chained. Up to now all my talk about wanting to be independent and competent and self-assured had just been talk. Brave talk, but talk nevertheless. The reassurance of the Emperor was all I needed. Now I was ready for the ultimate step.

At about eight o'clock we all gathered to head back to the caves. I couldn't have been more ready. The bus ride was very quiet. A sense of anticipation filled the air. When we reached the caves I looked up at the sky and noticed that the moon was not as full as it was during our previous evening ritual. The ground was rocky and I was already stumbling.

Don Riccardo set up his *mesa*. The crystals, the staffs, the shells, the stones . . . they were all there. We contributed our items to the mesa. Auriana came by and I handed over the crystal pendant. The caves were prepared, the candles lit, and don Riccardo began calling on the spirits of the four winds. Though I had been anxiously awaiting this ritual, I found myself distracted. I was concerned about Carole. Exhausted and beat, Alberto had nevertheless convinced her to come along. And I, too, was exhausted. But I'd been exhausted before. This was different. Maybe I was shielding myself from possible disappointment. Suppose nothing came to me in my three minutes. What if the guard at the Cave of the Light wouldn't let me pass? I also had some anxiety about swallowing more tobacco juice down my nose. Alberto hadn't said anything about it, and I was too fearful to ask if this was going to be part of the ritual.

One fear was put to rest early. The tobacco juice would not be a part of tonight's activities. We drank instead the mixture of San Pedro. It was bitter, but a bitterness I could live with. The tobacco mixture was something else.

Don Riccardo continued his ritual. He whistled a melodic tune, and his jet black hair was loose, resting gently on his shoulders. He wore an alpaca robe for the ceremony, and he shook his rattle while calling upon the spirits of the four winds.

We went into our separate meditations, and I was conscious of Alberto moving about our group, selecting one, then another, and leading them to the Cave of the Monkeys. My anxiety began to build again. I wasn't entirely there. My meditation was shallow, and I was afraid I would be spiritually not up to snuff when the time came for my shoulder to be tapped.

An eternity seemed to pass, then Alberto was beside me, resting a hand on my shoulder. He took my hand and led me up the rocky hill to the Cave of the Monkeys. There was a candle burning in the first chamber where one of the spirit guides sat as guardian to the cave. A candle was also burning in the second chamber. I left my offering and sat down to meditate in the half lotus position as instructed.

I concentrated. I called on the spirits, and asked for the jaguar to come to me that I could look into its eyes, into my reflected death. And as I meditated I was suddenly overcome with the tremendous sensation of floating. It was almost like an energy force around me, and I began to shiver. Something was happening to me.

The three minutes seemed to last forever, but then Alberto was calling to me that it was time to leave, another seeker was coming in. He took my hand and led me out of the cave. I was still floating, and it seemed that Alberto was floating, too. I looked down at his feet to make sure they were anchored to the ground, because I couldn't feel the rocky ground beneath me.

Before we reached the entrance to the Cave of the Light, Auriana materialized from the dark and blocked my way. She wore a headdress that was almost Egyptian.

"Why is it you desire to pass?" she said. Her eyes were piercing, her voice grave.

I had not rehearsed what I was going to say at this juncture. I had thought about it, but a smooth, glib, memorized speech would not come to me. I trusted that at the moment I would know what to do, what to say.

"It is time for me to step into my power," I said. "I am prepared to die and I am seeking enlightenment."

She hesitated a moment, her eyes burned into me like two black coals. Then she moved aside and let me pass. Alberto and I moved into the Cave of the Light, running our hands over the carved serpent.

Again, I went past the first candle, the spirit guide, and the second candle in the chamber beyond. I got down into the half lotus position and prepared for my meditation, but something happened. It was as though someone had gently pushed me back to a reclining position, so that I was flat on my back, staring up at the top of the cave. There was a slight opening in the rock and I felt a beam of energy coming down as clearly as one could feel the heat from a beam of sunlight. It came directly down to the center of my head, penetrating my third eye.

I lay there and let the sensation wash over me. It felt cold, and I began trembling uncontrollably, but it was not a cold that could be measured with thermostats. The cold was within rather than without. Whatever it was had rendered me almost incapable of movement. I felt pinned to the spot.

An hour seemed to pass, but I knew that it could only have been the allotted three minutes. Alberto's voice roused me, and I was aware that another needed to gain entrance to the cave. I was gently lifted up by some unseen force and walked out of the cave. Alberto stretched out his hand to me and I took it.

"What was that?" I managed to ask.

He only smiled, put two fingers to his lips, indicating silence, and we moved towards a stone not far from the cave.

I sat, and, with eyes wide open, concentrated on the brightest star in the Universe. I began to see swirls of energy, and these swirls transformed before my eyes into animals, then faces, then flashes of places in other times. I had the distinct impression of being pulled down by a kind of psychic quicksand, down out of the here and now and into a kind of collective unconscious, into the depths of my soul.

But I was conscious enough to know that these images were just illusions. Distractions. I knew that I had to let them pass and continue to look at the light.

As I struggled to free myself, I sank deeper and deeper. It was then that I realized the key was to not struggle at all. I simply had to maintain focus on the light, and not fight with the distractions. They would pass. The faces were frightening. They would roar from out of nowhere, like the distended images in a childish nightmare, and then be gone. It took all my will to ignore them.

I heard music in the distance, coming from the distant town. There was nothing between the town and where we were to absorb the sound. The music itself became part of the experience. I thought I was winning the battle, but just then the energy swarmed around me and pulled me down. I struggled to free myself. I struggled against the drowning.

Finally I knew I was going under. I called out to don Riccardo telepathically. "Help me!" I called. "I don't know how to get out of this!"

Then there was a sound, and with the sound something flashed to my right like a bolt of lightening. It was a horse, galloping through the sky. For a moment I thought it was my own power animal coming to rescue me, but then I realized no, it was don Riccardo. He had heard my cries for help.

The images dispelled, and I was able to concentrate freely on the light of the star. I was exhausted, but this did not keep me from rising up, up, up with grace and ease. An incredible lightness enveloped my body, and I rose with a smile on my face. I had weathered it. I had survived.

Then all was silent but for don Riccardo chanting softly in the background. I opened my eyes. He was bringing the ceremony to a close, and the members of the group were drifting back to the circle. Everything was gentle and slow, as though some power other than ourselves were lifting us up. I got to my feet and walked over, tears in my eyes, and I looked at the beings of light that surrounded me. These were the Masters. I had been here before. There wasn't the slightest doubt in my mind. I knew these Masters. I knew these beings of light. I watched them as they retreated over the horizon, felt the vibration of their presence as the ceremony came to a close.

I had come home. I had come home to the *naqual*. Chills ran up my spine and a great peace fell over me. This is what I've been homesick for. Dorothy clicking the heels of her slippers together. I felt the tears come down my cheeks.

I had come all the way to Peru to find my way back home.

CHAPTER ELEVEN

We made our way back to the bus in the dark. I was lost in my thoughts. We boarded the bus as in a dream and headed back down the mountain.

Alberto says there are two things a Shaman has to be wary of: fear, and the giggles. If fear doesn't get you, the giggles will. The bus had been severely ambushed by a case of the giggles. I couldn't join in. I didn't feel giddy. I felt as though my body was on the bus, but my spirit was somewhere else.

Back at the hotel Alberto announced that he had a small surprise for us. He swung open the heavy wooden gates of the room where we'd met earlier, and there before us was spread the most incredible banquet of pies and cakes and wines I had ever seen. The group dove into the feast, laughing and ravenous. Except me. It all seemed oddly decadent, and I felt so disconnected I couldn't imagine wanting to eat.

While standing in the corner trying to figure out which century I was living in, Ralph came over to ask what was wrong. "I'm having a hard time connecting with my body," I told him.

He nodded. "This sounds like a job for my power duck."

Ralph's power duck was a little rubber duck that belonged to his kids back home. He'd brought it with him so he could feel his family close. He worked on my chakras with the power duck and as silly as it seemed, I began to reconnect.

"Thank you," I said.

He smiled, put the duck back in his pocket. "Never fails."

The party continued on. An Andean minstrel band came in playing the most beautiful and melodic music I had ever heard. I smiled, and gradually let myself go.

Alberto had always stressed the point that the true Shaman can never take himself too seriously. They are always looking to balance the forces of light and dark. What better way to balance out the intense seriousness of the ritual with a party? It was perfect. Before I knew it, I was swept up in the lighter side of this initiation, and was out dancing to the music.

After an hour or so Alberto finally clapped his hands and said it was time to get some rest. We had to (what else?) get up early the next morning, and we were pushing it already. I gathered up my things and went to my room.

As I was getting ready for bed Carole came into the room. At least, it was somebody in Carole's body. Something had happened to her. Gone was the deathly ill woman who worried about keeping up with the rest of the group.

She fluttered excitedly around the room like a butterfly, full of happiness and brimming with good health. I gazed at her, speechless.

"How was your night?" she asked.

"<u>My</u> night? What about <u>your</u> night?"

"Well," Carole beamed. "I think I've finally arrived!"

I sat up in bed, excited. "What do you mean?"

"I finally had a spiritual experience," she said. Her face was glowing. She was hardly able to contain herself. "Up on the mountain, in the middle of my meditation . . ." she paused to let the drama of her words build. "I heard music! Actual music! Right in the middle of my meditation!"

Cuzco seen from Sacsayhuman.

My heart sank. "Carole, that was the music from the village. Real music. We all heard it."

Carole's smile began to fade. "Real music?"

"Yes. It's like . . . it's like listening to music drifting across a lake. There was nothing to stop it."

"So it didn't come from the cosmos?"

"No. Unless you consider Cuzco the cosmos, which might, in fact, be true."

Carole's eyes fell to the floor and she dropped, disheartened, onto her bed. "So much for my spiritual connection."

I got up and sat down next to her on her bed. "It's not that big a deal," I comforted.

"The hardest part about following this path is finding it to begin with," she said.

"Carole!" I stood up and held out both arms in her direction. "Look at you! You look ten years younger! Are you going to try to tell me you didn't have a significant experience tonight? So what if the music you heard was actual music. You heard music, and it moved something in you, and that's the important thing."

"I guess you're right," she said.

"Of course I'm right. Stop minimizing your experience."

"Tell me something," Carole said, a slow smile beginning to spread across her face. "How can you be so sure that the music I was hearing was the music from Cuzco?"

That one stopped me. "I can't Carole," I smiled at last. "I can't."

Our conversation came to a close and I crawled in to bed. It was important to sleep, but my mind was racing. Images flashed before my eyes. For a while it bothered me because I knew I had to get up in just a few hours, but then I realized it didn't matter if I was awake or asleep. It was all the same. I saw the same things whether my eyes were opened or closed.

Then, just when I thought I might be overtaken by slumber, a woman came to me. It was the same woman who'd come to me with the Empress tarot card. Her lips began to move, but I didn't hear words. That was when I realized I wasn't in my body at all. My awareness had broken out of the shackles of flesh and bone. I wasn't in my body, and it was as though this woman could hear every thought, because it was with thought that we communicated.

"Come with me," she said. "I have much to show you tonight."

We journeyed together that night. How, in what form . . . these are questions I can't begin to answer. It was as though we were formless. The woman led me down pathways that revealed different lifetimes. I saw my own tree of life, the imprint of my lifetime upon my soul.

"You are a very old soul," she said to me, "and you had many, many lives. Come, let me show you."

The lives were as varied as the imagination could conceive. I saw myself in an advanced civilization, traveling across the universe at a fantastic speed . . . I found myself as a peasant girl. A knight took me to be his wench, and I felt it was my duty to serve him well. Ah, the reverberations of the past lifetimes! Then I came upon a place that looked like ancient Greece, in robes, before an altar. What did this mean? Had I been a healer before? Had I chosen a spiritual path in my distant and shadowy past?

"It's time to remember your past," the Empress said to me, reading my thoughts. "For it is your past that will lead you to your future."

The words were barely echoing in my consciousness when I found myself as an American Indian, again a woman in a powerless position. The lifetimes seemed to fluctuate between an existence of power and an existence of subservience. I understood that my present lifetime required a balance.

Finally, after the long night's journey, the Empress smiled and told me that was enough for one night. Very gently, I was covered by a blanket of darkness. I could no longer see, and at last drifted into sleep.

When the proverbial early-morning knock came at my hotel room door I groaned and rolled back over in bed. I could barely move, and the events of the previous night were hopelessly intermingled with my dreams. I wasn't sure what had happened and what was simply imagined.

I eventually got dressed, struggling in the shadow of Carole, who was still cheery and rested and looking like a million dollars. We had to catch a plane to Lima, then transfer to another plane that would take us to Trujillo, a coastal city in the north of Peru. This was where our journey would end, in the north, calling upon the spirit of the horse. Trujillo was also the home of don Riccardo, and we planned on spending some time with him and his family.

I dragged my luggage downstairs and continued on with the humdrum necessities of moving from one place to the next. I had the urge to run and grab Alberto and tell him about my experiences of the previous night. But I didn't. He was very busy, of course, and I still had some doubts. Maybe my experience wasn't all that unique. Or was it out of synch with the rest of the group, and I would be left feeling alone and alienated.

So I resisted running and grabbing Alberto. I couldn't have run anyway, so it was just as well.

The flight to Lima was almost on time, which was a miracle to rank right up there with the Cave of the Light. I wondered if Einstein, in his theory of time, had figured out why things move so slowly in South America in relation to New York.

But the punctuality miracle was short-lived. The flight from Lima to Trujillo was delayed over and over again for a variety of obscure reasons.

While waiting I had an opportunity to think about my role in all of this. I wasn't a Peruvian. I wasn't going to rent an apartment in Cuzco and set up shop. No, I was going to return to New York. And when I returned I was going to find all the confining boundaries I had fled from only a few short days ago. My challenge was going to be to live within that culture, within those limitations, and assimilate what I had come to know into my work.

My mind went back to a client I had dealt with several years earlier. He had come to mental health clinic where I worked for treatment. He told the psychiatrist that he and his girlfriend were having the same dreams of themselves in another lifetime, and that he felt guided to paint by a source higher than himself. He was very anxious, and quite unsure as to how to deal with this.

He was diagnosed, naturally, as Paranoid Schizophrenic. In other words, someone out of touch with reality. Playing the role of the competent social worker, I stuck to the traditional psychotherapy. In my heart of hearts I knew what I wanted to do. I wanted to take him aside and say, look, you don't have a problem except putting your emotional well-being in the hands of this short-sighted psychiatrist. You should deal with your psychic experiences as legitimate phenomena -- as signs of emerging health, rather than sickness. But I didn't. In the name of being "professional," I fell in with the party line.

At last they called us to our plane. I picked up my baggage and thought of that man and hoped that he was doing okay now in spite of us. I had betrayed him, and myself. And as I walked towards my flight to Trujillo, I knew that I would never betray a client like that again.

While waiting for the flight, Alberto arranged for our group to have a private area in the airport. We passed the time doing the Tarot again, this time picking a card for someone else in the group. I chose for Auriana, and she seemed delighted and surprised that I had picked her. Madison chose one for me. She brought it over and set it on my lap. The card was called The Lovers.

"Perfect," I said. "It's like the joining of the Emperor and the Empress. A marriage. A union of opposites."

"Do you look at it literally?" Madison asked.

"Not really," I said. "To me, it means the merging of the two life forces, of parts within myself leading to a new birth. A new beginning. In New York I'd probably think it meant a new boyfriend. Down here . . . I don't know. It seems to represent the entire purpose of my trip."

CHAPTER TWELVE

By the time we reached Trujillo it was already evening. After seven hours waiting around the Lima airport, we were anxious to get to the Hotel de Tourista and get settled. After a solid night of deep and dreamless sleep, I woke up refreshed and alert. It was one of the few times somebody wasn't hammering on the door in the pre-dawn darkness.

Don Riccardo lived twenty minutes outside Trujillo, right on the water, and we were all anxious to meet his wife, Maria, and some of their fourteen children and grand children. We took a bus out to the small restaurant he owned. It was a stucco building with a dirt floor.

Again, the poverty was overwhelming, and the hordes of children who raced out to greet us at the bus only reconfirmed my concern for the future of countries like Peru. But such grim statistics were secondary to the joy don Riccardo got in introducing us to his family. We all went out to the beach and sat in the sand and the children jabbered to us endlessly in Spanish. After a few laughing attempts at translation, we fell into a warm and comfortable silence.

Maria prepared a traditional Peruvian dish called Ceviche, which is a pickled sea bass served with onions and vegetables. I'd seen don Riccardo and Alberto eating it in some of the restaurants we'd been to, but had refrained myself from indulging. But here I dove right in, and was surprised at how good it was. A little like the pickled herring my father used to buy for us kids during Sunday morning breakfast.

After the meal we all went outside, behind the restaurant, and stretched out in the grass beneath the mild Peruvian sun. Don Riccardo found a comfortable spot and began to talk to us about a diagnostic and healing process used by the Shaman. Alberto sat by his side and translated.

"In the West," he said. "Diagnosis and healing are two separate processes. When a Shaman works, they become one. Together. Inseparable. Within the process of diagnosing, you are also healing. The healing is not only of the body but of the mind and the spirit."

Don Riccardo called for a volunteer so that he could show us how a healing could be done with the use of a guinea pig. Carole's hand went up, and don Riccardo agreed to use her for the demonstration.

I was surprised when don Riccardo suddenly produced an actual, live guinea pig from a nearby cage. When he had said guinea pig, I thought he was using the general term for volunteer. But no. He meant a real, live guinea pig.

Don Riccardo explained that the guinea pig has an extremely high level of sensitivity, and has been used over the centuries for the purpose of diagnosis and healing. The spirit of the animal is asked if he will sacrifice himself for the noble cause, because it involves the execution of the guinea pig.

As he explained the process, don Riccardo took the guinea pig and began rubbing it all over Carole. She was suddenly not quite so happy about volunteering. I watched her take a deep breath and shut her eyes. As the guinea pig went through this process it did not fight and squirm and try to get away. It was almost as though the guinea pig itself was going into a trance. He became limp and relaxed in don Riccardo's hands.

Shamanic diagnosis via guinea pig.

"The sensitivity of the animal," don Riccardo explained. "Allows it to absorb whatever negative energy is in the body. If a person is suffering from black magic, the spine of the guinea pig will snap and the animal will die."

Ralph raised his hand. "What do you mean by black magic? Like voodoo?"

"Yes and no," Alberto said. "Black magic can be inflicted upon us from many sources."

I sat on my heels and thought of that day in Machu Picchu when don Riccardo had pulled what looked like black thread out of Carole's throat.

"And in that sense," Alberto went on, "black magic is something like voodoo. It is called different things in different parts of the world. But still, the worst black magic we do is the black magic that we do against ourselves.

We turn our own energy against us in order to create disease. Back home, in the United States, we refer to it as psychosomatic illness. We take care of the symptom and deem ourselves cured, when in reality the cause is still there to work against us."

What happened next I was not prepared for. After rubbing the guinea pig all over Carole's body, don Riccardo took a knife and cut the skin off the animal to examine the organs. I lurched back in horror as don Riccardo shook the blood of the guinea pig into a pail of water.

Ignoring the general shock of the group, don Riccardo methodically looked through the entrails of the guinea pig and nodded. "You have a problem with your gall bladder and your liver," he told Carole.

Carole confirmed this. She had known of it from tests done earlier in the States, but she had done nothing about it. Don Riccardo instructed one of his daughters, who was a herbologist, to prepare a herbal brew for Carole. Carole rose shakily, thanked don Riccardo for what he'd done, and we wandered back to the bus. It would be a short goodby, though, since we were all due to return to the same spot later in the evening for a fire ceremony.

We returned to our hotel and had a few hours to rest up before the next event, a trip to the temples of the Sun and Moon. Don Riccardo and his apprentices were already there, and they had created the symbol of a spiral on the ground, using rocks collected from an area between the temples of the Sun and the Moon.

Our group formed a circle around the spiral, and we began to chant, "oh ma kong, oh ma kong, oh ma kong..."

And as we chanted, we moved around the spiral in a clockwise direction. The spiral represented the journey to the center of the earth, and one by one we entered. At the center we were to face the East and raise our hands to the sky and then face the West again, holding our hands to the cosmos.

When it was my turn I walked through the opening of the spiral without any difficulty. I don't know what I was expecting, but I was prepared for anything. This trip taught me that, if nothing else. I made my way to the center and stood there, raising my hands above me, facing the East. I felt slightly dizzy as the energy penetrated my body. I felt wonderful, but when I turned to the West and repeated the gesture, I could feel the old nausea coming back. It was a heavy feeling. Burdensome. I slowly made my way out of the spiral and took my place with the rest of the group, breathing deeply. After a few minutes the sudden nausea had subsided.

I noticed that odd things tended to happen to everybody who entered the spiral. Carole made her way in and then froze. It was as though something had reached out and grabbed her. Don Riccardo saw what was happening and began chanting loudly, staring at her, motioning with his hands and rattle until she seemed to shirk off the coils that had bound her and was able to make her way back out.

When the ceremony ended I moved close to Carole and whispered urgently in her ear. "What happened out there?"

"I don't know," Carol said. "I just couldn't move. It was as simple as that. I just couldn't move."

Stone spiral.

I left it alone. For some things there are no logical explanations. No. Correct that. I was learning in Peru that for most things there are no logical explanations. Transformations can lead to changes that may be even more difficult for us to deal with. Don Riccardo asked that we pick up the rocks that formed the ceremony and to scatter them, leaving no trace of the spiral.

We went directly to don Riccardo's home for the fire ceremony. We had been told earlier to prepare for this ceremony by thinking about a part of ourselves that we wanted to transform and give up to the fire. Alberto advised us to make our selections carefully. This was not a game. If you decided to give up too big a piece of yourself, there could be consequences.

"Beware," he warned with a good-natured twinkle in his eye. "There is one problem in the world of the Shaman. You may get just what you ask for."

It was obvious to me what would be sacrificed to the fire. It was my fear, the fear that kept me from stepping fully into my power. I brought a stick with me that I had wrapped with black thread. The thread represented the black web which I have always created in my life to keep me bound and unable to burst free . . . my own black magic.

Don Riccardo and Alberto were preparing the wood for the fire while the rest of us took seats in a circle around the pit.

"This is a transformational fire," Alberto explained. "Don Riccardo will call upon the energies from the streams that run deep under the earth. These are our transformational energies. We will call upon the spirits of the four winds to accept our offerings. We will know the offerings have been accepted when the fire turns into a friendly fire. We will put our hands through the fire three times, touching our foreheads, our hearts, and our stomachs. In this way we light the fire within. And our hands will not burn."

Alberto walked clockwise around the circle, pouring water as a circle of protection. Then, holding a rattle in one hand and a sword in the other, don Riccardo began calling upon the spirits of the four winds. He blew a mouthful of red wine in each direction. It represented our blood returning to mother Earth, and in front of the fire it was a very dramatic moment. I felt my very body altered. Then we began to chant. It was an old Indian chant that we had learned earlier in the day, a chant specifically for this ceremony.

"Nichi tai tai...En U I...Ora nikka, ora nikka...

Hey, hey...Hey, hey...Oh I"

The chant began to transport me. I drifted in and out of an easy world where faces and people changed from moment to moment. Then things became more focused. I suddenly realized that I was seeing out of the eyes of an Indian squaw. I was the squaw, and I was pregnant. The son of the Chief was the father. It was vaguely reminiscent of the experience I'd had in the Cave of the Monkeys. It seemed lifetimes ago.

We chanted for an hour, and gradually I noticed the flame of the fire turn blue. This was a sign that the fire had become friendly. One by one we approached, knelt before it, and put our offerings into the flame. Then we passed our hands through the fire as don Riccardo had instructed.

I was nervous, but as my offering burned I asked the spirits to allow me to break through my fears. The fire was simply a tangible example of what I had shied away from my whole life. Let me pass my hand through the danger. Let me turn my greatest fear into my greatest asset.

I placed my hands in the center of the flames. A feeling of relief swept through me. It felt as though I had stepped into a lukewarm bath. I brought my hands out and touched my forehead, then brought the warmth of the flame to my heart. Then, again, I put my hands into the depth of the heat, held them there a few seconds, bathing in the baptismal fire. Then I brought the friendly fire to my stomach. It didn't hurt. It hadn't burned me. I took a deep breath and stayed for a moment to thank the spirits for accepting my offering. Then I slowly got up and made my way back to my place in the circle.

We watched until the fire died. Then we watched some more. When there was nothing more to watch we all slowly got up in silence, and departed.

CHAPTER THIRTEEN

The last stage of the initiation process was finally before us. The trip, barely two weeks old, had seemed to me a lifetime. My endurance had been pushed and pushed and then pushed some more, and each time I believed I had reached my limit. Yet each time I had found the wherewithal to dig deeper.

The initiation itself was to take place at a lagoon, a two-hour drive south of Trujillo. This was the power spot where Shamans had brought their students for centuries. The bus ride, as always, was long and uncomfortable. It was midday before we arrived at the lagoon.

It was a cool day, and walked through the sand to the lagoon and gathered in a horse-shoe formation, facing the water. The Shamans really knew how to pick their initiation spots. The lagoon was beautiful, sunlight glinting off the peaceful water. A gentle breeze barely rippled the surface of the lagoon.

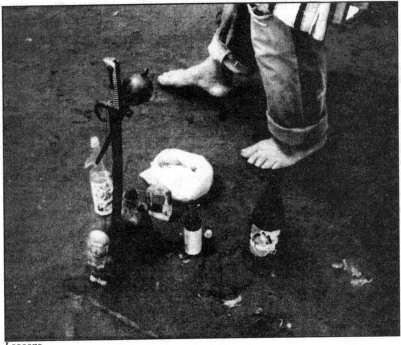

Lagoons

Don Riccardo began the ritual. He stood at the edge of the lagoon and pushed his sword into the sand. Then Alberto waded off shore, into the lagoon, and stuck three tall sticks into the water. These sticks were to symbolize the place where our physical world ended and where the world of the spirit began.

Don Riccardo shook his rattle and whistled and called upon the spirits of the Four Winds. It was a call to protect us, to open to us, and though I couldn't understand the language, I felt fully the power of his conviction.

The ritual process itself was very much like a baptismal. Each of us had to walk out into the lagoon. It was cold, and I felt myself begin to tense up. Yet another example of my tendency to pull back from that which would threaten my comfort or my safety. But this time I wasn't going to let it happen. This time I was going to shrug off the fears I had carried around with me for far too long. I thought of my sore throats, my achy bones, my tendency to pamper my illnesses beneath the safe blankets of home. No. Alberto was right. The worst black magic is the black magic we do to ourselves.

When it was my turn I went out into the water without fear or trepidation. This was the moment of my life . . . all I had been working for and thinking about. I was given a bit of lime with sugar, and I was to bite into it. The bitter and the sweet of life. The water was above my waist, but it wasn't nearly as cold as I had feared.

We were instructed beforehand to bring an offering to give of ourselves and leave in the lagoon. I had taken some strands of my hair and had wrapped them around a pebble. Now I took the pebble and threw it into the center of the lagoon. As long as a part of me remained in the lagoon, my spirit would be guarded.

I dropped quickly down into the water and then came right back up again. My body was shivering, but it didn't matter. I marched out of the water and went directly to don Riccardo.

He looked at me, then cleansed my spirit by blowing a mouthful of herbs upon my body. With his sword, he touched the energy points on my body, cutting me loose from my past. He took my hand and started spinning me around. He spun so fast that I fell to the ground, rolling in the earth. It was my rebirth, my new beginning. This time, my mother is the earth.

I went back out into the lagoon, this time running, and dove deep into the cold, clear water. Then I came back to don Riccardo, who shook his rattle around me body and offered prayers to the spirits. I turned, dripping the sacred waters, and went back to my place in the group.

In the evening we celebrated our initiation. It was to be held at the Temple of the Sun and Moon, and I was both thrilled and exhausted. A part of me wanted this to go on forever, but an equally strong part wanted very much to be back in New York, in my apartment, and having a good rest.

Home. That was a joke. Where was home? I didn't even know what that meant anymore, because through this journey I had discovered my true home. Not Peru, but the home of my spirit. The *Naqual*.

On the bus don Riccardo sat at the front and spoke to us. "This could be dangerous," he said. "So we must be sure to come to this ceremony pure of heart and with good intentions as Shamans, or there will be consequences for each of us to face."

I wondered how a celebration could be dangerous, but before I could pursue my thoughts we were there. The stone wall of the temple suddenly filled the front window of the bus.

We entered the gates of the temple, again in silence and with our flashlights turned off. The sky was bright with stars, and that was all the light we needed.

For several minutes we wound through the maze of walls until at last we found an open space and don Riccardo began to set up his *mesa*. I watched with a feeling of contentment. I remembered how strange the whole ceremony had seemed at the beginning. Now it was as natural and familiar as the sun coming up in the East.

My feeling of contentment melted, however, when I saw don Riccardo begin to drink the vile tobacco concoction through his nose. I dreaded the possibility of having to go through that again. Even don Riccardo gagged on the mixture. He had to drink it seven times, his assistants four. And though I hoped one day to be honored enough to be his assistant, this was one aspect of the job I was ready to do without. As it was, I only had to take one shell full of the mixture. I watched the others in the group go up, one by one, and take the drink. None of them seemed to have much problem with it. I squirmed where I sat. This was supposed to be a celebration. Instead it was like sitting in the dentist's waiting-room. The anticipation of what was to come was far worse than the actual event.

When it was my turn I looked at Carole sitting next to me and she gave me a thumbs-up.

"It can't be as bad as last time," I said.

"You'll be fine," she said. "You'll be just fine."

Like a prisoner walking to the executioner, I approached don Riccardo. Get it over with. Take it like a big girl and stagger back and try to throw up in private. I put the tobacco mixture to my nose and drank.

I waited for a moment, stunned. Where was the nausea? Where was the bile rising in my throat? The mixture had gone down without a hitch. I'd felt nothing.

Stunned, I made my way back to the group. Something had changed. Nobody in particular had noticed it, but something had changed. Perhaps the woman from Long Island had made the leap. Had catapulted herself out of the physical level and into something spiritual. The stomach doesn't lie.

When everyone had partaken of the tobacco mixture, don Riccardo began the final ritual by calling on the Spirits of the Four Winds. He chanted and shook his rattle. Spit perfume in the air and lit the sacred tobacco. Waved his sword through the air. With each wave of the sword he cut through the energy fields in the four directions that keep us connected to our material world. He -- and the group -- were to walk between the worlds.

When don Riccardo felt the time was right, we were each asked to do the dance of the Four Winds. The dance would connect us to each of the four directions. As each person took their turn, don Riccardo handed them a power staff.

Alberto was first. Power staff in hand, he stepped inside the circle. It was a beautiful dance -- graceful, self-assured, rhythmic. As Alberto reached each of the four directions he jumped into the air, spun, and continued on. First counter-clockwise, then the other direction, he continued on till ending up back in front of don Riccardo.

I was looking forward to my turn to do the dance of the Four Winds. Dancing was like a meditation for me. Something I felt completely comfortable with. So much of what I had been through was so totally alien. When the ritual turned to dance, I felt on safe ground.

I approached don Riccardo and he handed me one of his power staffs. As I gripped the staff I suddenly realized something that shook me to my foundations. The staff was gripping me. It took me off, around in the circle.

Once, twice, three times, the staff pulled me through the dance of the Four Winds. Gone was the residual egocentric notion that "I" was a good dancer, that "I" could do this well. That "I" would have no problem. There was no "I" here. Only the spirit, and the ways of the Shaman.

I spun and turned and dance with grace and ease. It was the cat dancing through me. Several times while watching the others I had feared that when my turn came I would whirl out of the circle and bump into people, but now that thought was as distant as the craters of the moon. I gave in to the experience, and the experience itself watched out for me.

At last I stopped, out of breath, and faced don Riccardo. I handed him back his power staff, and in return he gave me a crystal. It was the quartz crystal that had been charged at each ritual along the journey. I was to always have it close. It would keep me connected to these great and ancient places.

When the dance had been completed, Alberto told us to walk along the temple walls and find a comfortable place where we could meditate. Then we were to call upon the spirit of the North, represented by the horse, and ask him to bring us higher knowledge.

I found my spot, sat down, and felt the crystal pulsating in my hand as I called upon the horse. "Come close," I cried out silently. "Come closer and take me to the crystal cave where the masters sit."

The horse came. As in a dream, it swept down from the clouds and carried me off. For a long time we flew, through time and space, away . . . a cave appeared before us, and in the cave there were people. A man in a long robe greeted me at the entrance and led me in. He spoke, and his voice was deep and hypnotic.

"You have five spirit guides," he said.

Five images appeared before me, and I recognized some of them from my previous meditations.

"What is their purpose?" I said.

"They are linked with your chakras," the man said. "Their purpose you will come to know. Everything you need to know will be taught you directly by the masters. You have little need of a teacher in the material world. You will learn as you sleep. What others call a sleep will be, for you, a wakefulness. But I will show you your power animals, and I will explain which chakras they are connected to."

Suddenly I was brought out of my meditation. Someone was crying and gagging, and for a moment I couldn't distinguish if it was real or imaginary. Then I realized it was Lourdes. She was only a few feet away from me and seemed very sick. I began to move towards her, but don Riccardo's apprentices told me to stay where I was.

I tried to return to the cave, to call the horse, but it was impossible. Lourdes was getting sicker and sicker, and I noticed other members of the group were also having trouble concentrating. At last the ritual came to an end. Lourdes was so sick she had to be carried to the bus, and the ride back to Trujillo was a sober one. Silent, except for Lourdes in the back, softly crying.

I found myself wondering at the quality of health care in this part of Peru, where we would find a hospital, and so on. But as the bus drew nearer and nearer the town, Lourdes grew stronger and stronger. By the time we reached the hotel she was perfectly fine.

Alberto sat next to me, and I asked him how such a remarkable turnabout could take place.

"I think Lourdes is still too much in her head," Alberto said. "She did not come to the ceremony with a knowing in her heart of the path she wanted to follow. So when we were close to the spiritual center, she was at her sickest. As we returned to the physical world, she grew well."

We talked a bit more, then Alberto said goodnight and went off. I simply sat for awhile and closed my eyes and rested. I was exhausted. The ceremony was the last ritual we would do together as a group. A great sadness came over me, but it was a sadness tempered by the knowledge that the doors were only just now opening. The greater work was still ahead, and there would be many more groups. At last I stood and wandered off to bed.

The next morning dawned bright and beautiful. I took a walk in the garden and recognized some of don Riccardo's sculptures. They reflected just how sensitive a man he was. The detail and expression was magnificent, particularly on the bust he'd done of his wife, Maria.

While admiring the work I heard Alberto calling to all of us to reassemble. Everyone slowly walked over and found a seat on the grass, forming a circle. The sadness of the previous night welled up in me again. This would probably be our last formal meeting as a group, as a tribe.

"Our trip is coming to an end," Alberto said. "But this is only the beginning of your initiation. We must all make a decision within the next thirteen full moons as to whether or not we accept the invitation to become a Shaman. When you go home you must complete your own fire ceremony. When you have done that, and continued for thirteen full moons, you have made the decision to become a Shaman."

"What happens then?" somebody asked.

"It is up to you," Alberto answered. "But it must always be kept in mind how serious this decision is. This is not like a job that you quit or get fired from. Once you have made your commitment, you can't take it back."

The same voice. "Why not?"

"Because your Karma is now instantaneous. Before, the laws of Karma that applied were different. It was the Karma of learning a lesson from lifetime to lifetime. But now, as a Shaman, the consequences of your actions are immediate, and if you fall, you fall hard.

"Alberto shifted on the grass and looked out past us. "I know what you are thinking," he said. "How can a fellow in a three-piece suit be a Shaman. You have grown accustomed to this wild man, stripped to the waist, spitting magical juices into the Peruvian sky. But it doesn't work that way. Don Riccardo had a vision several years ago that the new Shamans would come from the West. The white man would be the new caretaker of the Earth."

"How could that be?"

I finally recognized the voice that was asking all the questions. It was Ralph.

"In the past," Alberto said. "Immortality was maintained by the species, but death came to the individual. As one generation would die, the species would change through the next generation. The sick and weak would die off, and the species was kept strong and pure. The evolutionary process happened naturally, and quickly. But technology has changed all that. Now those that would have died still live. I, myself, was a sickly child and would have died in another era. Don't get me wrong. I'm glad to be alive, but the fact remains that technology has cut our connection with nature. We don't have the time anymore to wait for evolution to make us conscious. It is the individual who must make the leap, not the generation. We, as Shamans, the new caretakers of the Earth, must guide our own species through future sight and not wait for the next generation. We have no time to waste."

"Do you mean nuclear war?" Ralph said, picking at a blade of grass.

"That is the most apparent danger, yes," Alberto said. "But there are many other reasons for not wasting time. Our natural resources are being depleted. We must learn in this lifetime to become conscious. For living, and for dying."

Ralph looked puzzled. "Dying?"

"Yes," Alberto said, gazing out at all of us in the group. "How many of you have friends or relatives that died in a hospital bed with tubes up their noses, and with drugs that made them drowsy and disoriented?"

All of us raised our hands.

"There! Then you know what I mean. Those people did not die consciously. They are so disoriented they don't even know they're dead. What a terrible thing to deny someone."

Then Alberto told us an incredible story of how his grandmother had died in just such a fashion, medicated senseless. Later Alberto had gone to Brazil and a friend of his who was a psychic medium began to speak in Spanish, not her native language. Alberto realized it was his grandmother speaking through the woman. She was sad and confused and didn't know where she was. Since she was able to talk to Alberto, she assumed she was alive. Alberto had to tell her no, that she was not in her own body, not in her own time. The medium and healers who were present were able to heal her and free her.

"I could hear her," Alberto said. "She was so filled with joy that she was at last able to rid herself of the notion of her physical body and move on into the light."

Listening to Alberto, I was able to look at my own father's death in a different way. He had gone down immediately, no warning, from a heart attack. Death had been instantaneous. Up till now I had always thought of it as a tragedy. Now I realized how fortunate he was to have been spared the medications that disorient one about their leavetaking.

We moved on to other things, and the excited talk of the group filled the sun-splashed garden. With all of this talk about death, I was definitely glad to be alive, to feel the warmth upon my face.

"I'm afraid I won't be able to heal people," Carole said. "I just don't feel I have the capabilities."

"A Shaman is not just a healer," Alberto said. "There are many different kinds of Shamans. I don't choose to heal. I can do it if I need to, but my position is more one of teaching. Some are Shamans of knowledge. Some have clear visions and build organizations to heal the planet. Each Shaman has a specialty which involves doing the work of one of the four directions."

For the last time, Alberto took out the Tarot cards. We were told to look at them face up, and choose one that would represent a goal we were working towards. I chose the Star. It had beautiful swirling colors emanating from the star, and a woman holding two cups, one above and one below. I stared at the card till I felt myself drawn deeper into it, so deep I could hear the voice of the woman. I don't know who the woman is, but she has guided me through the journey.

"You will begin to receive teachings directly from the center of the light," she said. "You will be bathed in the light as you sleep and will travel far beyond that which you have already journeyed. You will be shown the love in the light and will follow in the tradition of those who have preceded you for centuries. Your journey will consist of three parts. First, you will journey with the purpose of reconnecting to the source of your energy. You will accomplish this through your meditation and a cleansing process. You have been experiencing the first step of this journey. The cleansing opened you up to the higher knowledge and the power source. Second, you will proceed to the next level. This consists of travel and exploration. The travel is on many levels. You will be obtaining new ability, knowledge, and power beyond which you have known in the past. You will learn of new worlds and you will bring back this knowledge which will be followed by scientific exploration. Your travel will allow you to share with others who travel from different parts of your galaxy and beyond."

I listened with amazement and disbelief, struggling to put aside my ego and become one with her.

"You will learn much from your travels," she continued. "The earthly travels will parallel the spiritual travels. All will come together in time. All will make sense. Do not judge or try to understand that which you cannot from your limited perspective. Let it be, and be your experience in the moment."

"And third, the final leg of the journey involves transcendence. You will begin to achieve this within the later years of your present life on earth. Transcendence means that there will no longer be a differentiation between your physical and your spiritual being. Your mind, or your ego, will give itself up. The struggle will no longer be as such. You will be at peace with your existence on all levels and will easily integrate the intellectual knowledge and the emotional and spiritual knowing."

"You will transcend the distinctions made by man on a personal and societal level. Man has created false boundaries in order to provide a structure and a frame of reference. Your reference point will be your soul, and the soul knows no boundaries."

"Be open. Do not judge. Accept and love. All will come to you. You are love. Love is within you. We are all one and love is within us all. Look only to the light and you will guided on a journey that will lead you back to yourself." I listened to her words, deep into the meditation.

"Look to the light, my child," she continued. *"All else will find its place. Bathe in the light and feel it shine from within. Follow your heart and your direction will be clear. You will know the steps to take along the way. If you are open to opportunity, it will present itself to you."*

I sat in silence as my meditation came to an end.

Then the group sat together and talked of their experiences in the various rituals. I felt the terrible limitations of words. These were experiences that couldn't be reduced to adverbs, adjectives, and nouns.

But as they spoke something occurred to me. Something critical. I had left my offering, my crystal, in the wrong cave. I was supposed to leave it in the Cave of the Light, but instead had deposited it in the Cave of the Monkeys. How could I have been so stupid?

For a moment I felt a great unease. I had planned so carefully, I had taken such pains to be sure that everything went exactly right.

I got up and moved away from the rest of the group. Then something else occurred to me. Had my mistake disrupted or lessened in any way the intensity of my experience? No, it hadn't. Not at all. I had just learned another Shamanic lesson. It was not necessarily what you did, but the intent with which you did things that was important. It was everything. A person with bad intent who memorized all the numbers and where to put what was no more a Shaman than the man in the moon.

At last it was time to say good-bye to don Riccardo. Ralph and Bruce proposed that the group band together and start a fund to finance don Riccardo's artwork. We would buy a kiln so that he might be more prolific. It would also help him to start a school in town, to teach the children his skill as an artisan.

When it came time for me to say good-bye, I could barely hold the tears back. I threw my arms around him and gave him a big kiss on the cheek. I had to stretch as far as I could in order to get around his big belly. He hugged me tightly, then let go. A Shaman never says good-bye. He will always see you again.

Then Auriana came up to me. "This is for you," she said. I looked at her gift. It was one of her earrings with the symbol of the Pachamama. "Wear this at the fire ceremony," she said. "And it will keep us connected."

Later, when it was time to get our luggage, Auriana came up behind me and put her hand on my shoulder.

"I'll see you in the fire," she said.

"Yes," I replied. "I will see you in the fire."

CHAPTER FOURTEEN

It was nine o'clock before we finally dragged ourselves into the Hotel Bolivar. The plane had been two and a half hours late taking off from Trujillo. The plane had been out of fuel and they couldn't find the man with the gas key. Peru.

But it was good for me. As a New Yorker, I had a very under-developed skill for patience. This trip taught me to sit back, relax, let things unfold as they will. Live in the moment.

Alberto had planned for us all to go out to dinner for our last night together. Though it was late, Alberto insisted that we needed to go regardless. The House of the Counts was, as Alberto boasted, the finest restaurant in all of South America. Several in our group didn't care. They were beat, and straggled up to their rooms for a long night's sleep. My inclination was to do the same, but I put my exhaustion aside and decided to go. What the hell. Live for the moment. There would be plenty of time back home to rest. The finest restaurant in South America was a long ways from Long Island.

The restaurant was like stepping into a castle, and I was glad I had changed into the one good dress I had brought along for the trip. Heavy wooden doors opened into a large entranceway with marble floors, high ceilings, leather Spanish love seats, and high-back chairs. A suit of armor stood guard at the door.

The Pisco Sours kept flowing. There was no dance floor, but that didn't keep us from dancing to the piano music. Then we went to our private room and drank wine and talked and laughed more than we should. Release was necessary and healthy. We had all been through so much together. There was no formality, no numbers, no rituals to concentrate on. Just food. Food, and more food. Forks were everywhere as everyone sampled everything. It was every man for himself.

We tried to imitate don Riccardo's whistle, and, of course, none of us could. I found myself glancing down at Carole, who endured the whistling with a tight, sheltered smile. I didn't know how far she had come towards overcoming this obstacle, and it was ironic that at this moment of celebration they should bring the issue of the whistling back in.

"Wait a minute!" Alberto cried. "I think Vicki has it!" Vicki stood and duplicated don Riccardo's whistle. It was very, very close, and we all roared our approval.

Then Alberto stood up. "I think I have it, too."

We all waited in breathless anticipation. He pressed his lips together and forced the sound through his lips. Clunk. It sounded like a kazoo. A very bad kazoo. He finished, bowed deeply to his audience, and took his seat. We all roared with laughter.

Ah, the paradox of Shamanism. I finally understood. To find that place of balance within, you must connect to the light as well to the dark, to the frivolous as well as to the serious. The whole spectrum. Encompass the multi-faceted panorama of human existence. The intensity of the whole Shamanic journey had culminated into a group of rowdy, hysterical, let-it-all-hang-out people who carried on beyond exhaustion into the wee hours of the morning.

As we left and felt the cool night air on our faces, I thought of how wonderful Lima was, and how different my perception was from the first day off the plane from Miami. I was no longer aware of the dinginess of the city. My own inner peace and appreciation for the beauty of Peru transcended the appearance of poverty. I took a deep breath, way down deep into my lungs, and tried to hold onto Peru just a little bit longer.

Vicki came out of the restaurant and stood next to me and together we gazed up at the sky full of stars.

"Isn't this a perfect way to end it?" I said.

"The end?" she said, and looked me seriously in the eyes. "You haven't seen anything yet. This is only the beginning."

Then she turned and walked away and left me there alone. Just me, and the blazing sweep of the Southern sky. Vicki was right. This was only the beginning.

CHAPTER FIFTEEN

Re-entry into ordinary reality wasn't without its bumps and bruises. Almost at the exact moment of arriving home, I broke into a fever and simply collapsed in bed for a few days. It might have been the release of stress after Peru, or the expectation of stress now that I was back, but whatever it was had stretched me out.

For six weeks all I wanted to do was sleep. I was growing more and more concerned until suddenly, one morning, I woke with a powerful surge of energy. The time had come to make a physical manifestation of the energy I had experienced on a spiritual level down south. It was time to come out of the closet. It was time to follow the Shamanic path in the here and now.

Just before leaving Peru an idea had come to me . . . a vision, almost. Or rather, the remembrance of a vision, because I had seen it before at Machu Picchu. I saw myself back in New York, and I saw Alberto there, too. A class of some sort was going on. A workshop, and he and I were both an integral part of it. I had mentioned this to Carole, and we'd plotted in a haphazard way to start some sort of organization once we got back. We even ran it past Alberto to see if he would be interested in being a guest speaker. He smiled broadly and said of course.

Now was the time to put that far-off Peruvian dream into reality. Carole and I began to do presentations on our Shamanic Journey of Initiation for the clinical staff in our hospital. The response was overwhelmingly positive. We drew parallels between the Social Worker and the Shaman, and demonstrated to our colleagues that the two disciplines were very much the same. It was just a matter of making the spiritual leap to integrate the two.

We recruited a friend -- a well-respected social worker named Maggi -- and went to work organizing our group. The response was simply too huge for Carole and me to handle. I was suddenly running a psychic hotline for spiritually distressed social workers.

We met, drew up plans and strategy. We had to nail down locations, plan publicity, bring it together so it wouldn't be a haphazard, well-intentioned start doomed to fail because of lack of attention to details. I thought of don Riccardo and his meticulous attention to his *"mesa."* It was no different here.

We decided to call our organization L.I.G.H.T., an acronym for the Long Island Group for Holistic Therapies, and within months the mailing list had grown enormously. Many of the names on our list were of professionals in the mental health field. Every once in awhile Carole and I would simply look at each other from across a table during one of the jam-packed sessions and simply smile and shake our heads. It was happening. It was truly happening.

93

In February my excitement rose. The first major workshop was due to be presented by L.I.G.H.T., and Alberto was coming out from California to give it. This was the first real connection to my Peru experience since the incredible events of fall, and I was thrilled at the notion of spending some time with Alberto. On the phone I invited him to stay in my house, and he accepted. Then I warned him that he ran the risk of me locking him in until he taught me everything he knew. Alberto laughed, said he'd take that chance, and hung up.

The weekend of the actual conference was utter chaos. Alberto was still operating on Peruvian time, and we cut the timing so close it added a dozen gray hairs to my head. Just before the workshop was to begin, while Alberto, his girlfriend Angelika, and I were having dinner at my home, I took out a very special bottle of red wine I had been saving for his visit. Alberto slowly swirled the wine around the rim of his glass.

"A toast," he said.

"To friends," I said, raising my glass as well.

"To L.I.G.H.T.," Alberto continued. "And to a successful workshop."

We drank, and I felt my heart race with excitement. I felt that I wasn't a confused, stumbling novice any longer. That Alberto was not looking at me with the same eyes as he had when I came bumbling off that first plane in Miami, full of apprehension and nervousness. The fact that he had come out all the way from California indicated that he saw me differently now. He was taking me seriously.

Then I put down the wine and smiled to myself. Why are you doing this, I said to myself. Maybe it was ME who was seeing myself differently. Maybe Alberto hadn't taken a step down from the pedestal to look me eye-to-eye. Maybe I was the one who took a step up.

Alberto's workshop was a stunning success. And I remember standing off to one side while he spoke, and looking at the faces of those who listened with the same flicker of fascination and wonder that I had not too many years ago. And I thought of the vision I'd had at Machu Picchu. I had seen a group of people sitting in a semi-circle listening to Alberto speak. These were the people. These were the faces. I smiled to myself and thanked the Eagle. It had helped me create a vision for myself. That was the hard part. But once the vision was clear, it was only a matter of implementing it, of being true to it, of seeing that it is manifested in the tangible world.

I thought of something that Sadie had said to me that day in Machu Picchu as she took my hand and looked into my palm.

"The only thing that can stop you from achieving" she had said, "is you."

Maybe, I thought, it was no more complicated than that. Then I turned my attention back on Alberto. On the hopeful faces lining him in a semi-circle.

THE END

Stairway, Machu Picchu.